BREA [barcode: D0862183]

"In this over-connected worl[d] ... yond platitudes, passing niceties, an ... ...ner sometime,' yet we're also too old to pass a ... ...ng 'Will you be my friend?'" By inviting us to join Jesus and his disciples at the Passover supper, Jessica Herberger offers us a biblical roadmap to discovering true friendship and building our own life-giving Breaking Bread Community. This book changed how I view friendship in general, but more importantly, how I view my own friendships."

—**Niki Hardy**, church planter and author of *Breathe Again*

"Jessica is a new friend for me, but her words connect me to my oldest and dearest friend, Jesus. For the past few years, I've been fascinated with the Last Supper and the last few hours of Jesus's life, and this incredible book helped shine more light on how this meal can still shift everything for us today. Grab this book, grab your friends, get around a table, and let it change your life."

—**Jess Connolly**, author of *You Are the Girl for the Job* and *Take It Too Far*

"Sitting around our small group time at a recent women's retreat, there was a common thread of isolation and loneliness. Many tears were shed over the longing to be in community and the helplessness of not knowing where or how to find it. Jessica Herberger understands our pain and lovingly offers biblical and practical hope. Jessica is relatable and wise, and *Break Bread Together* will spur you towards togetherness in a way that your heart desperately needs!"

—**Maria Furlough**, author of *Confident Moms, Confident Daughters* and *Breaking the Fear Cycle*

"For anyone who is craving more connection and community, this book is a must-read. It is encouraging and inspiring, and will help you create more meaningful relationships. Jessica gently teaches you how to serve and receive well and how to prioritize the friendships that you desire to prioritize. A delightful read!"

—**Morgan Tyree**, author of *Take Back Your Time* and founder of Morganize with Me

"Whether you're longing for one true friend or simply want to take your existing friendships deeper, Jessica is a worthy guide. With relatable stories from her own adventures in friendship and insightful glances at Jesus's closest friendships, you'll find just the encouragement you need to take the next step in forging beautiful, life-changing relationships."

—**Asheritah Ciuciu,** founder of One Thing Alone Ministries and author of *Uncovering the Love of Jesus*

"*Break Bread Together* is a kind-hearted invitation to follow Jesus and his closest friends around the table at the Last Supper, where we can learn how to interact with friends, how to serve them and receive service, and how to handle conflict. Jessica shows us the way to authentic and transformational friendships. Her open-handed stories unwrap our core needs. Every woman can benefit from this book whether you are setting the table or joining one already set for you. It's our time to know and reach out to the people God has called us to sit with and serve."

—**Blythe Daniel,** literary agent at The Blythe Daniel Agency and author of *Mended: Restoring the Hearts of Mothers and Daughters*

"You've been invited to the table! In a world where we're prone to retreat into our devices, Jessica Herberger invites us into community. She pulls out a chair at the table and welcomes us, not just to sit down but to draw near and break bread together. By looking through the lens of the Last Supper, she offers a fresh perspective, giving us courage to be brave and pursue friendships on a whole new level."

—**Betsy Pendergrass,** writer, speaker, and gatherer at www.gatheringaround.com

BREAK BREAD
Together

BREAK BREAD
Together

FINDING TRUE FRIENDSHIP AT THE LAST SUPPER

JESSICA HERBERGER

LEAFWOOD
P U B L I S H E R S
an imprint of Abilene Christian University Press

BREAK BREAD TOGETHER
Finding True Friendship at the Last Supper

LEAFWOOD
P U B L I S H E R S
an imprint of Abilene Christian University Press

Published in association with The Blythe Daniel Agency, Inc., PO Box 64197, Colorado Springs, CO 80962.

Library of Congress Cataloging-in-Publication Data
Names: Herberger, Jessica, 1977- author.
Title: Break bread together : finding true friendship at the Last Supper /
    Jessica Herberger.
Description: Abilene, Texas : Leafwood Publishers, [2020]
Identifiers: LCCN 2019057295 | ISBN 9781684264902 (trade paperback)
Subjects: LCSH: Communities—Religious aspects—Christianity. |
    Fellowship—Religious aspects—Christianity. | Friendship—Religious
    aspects—Christianity. | Intimacy (Psychology)—Religious
    aspects—Christianity. | Last Supper—Meditations.
Classification: LCC BV4517.5 .H48 2020 | DDC 241/.6762—dc23
LC record available at https://lccn.loc.gov/2019057295

Cover design by ThinkPen Design | Interior text design by Sandy Armstrong, Strong Design

Leafwood Publishers is an imprint of Abilene Christian University Press
ACU Box 29138, Abilene, Texas 79699

1-877-816-4455 | www.leafwoodpublishers.com

20 21 22 23 24 25 / 7 6 5 4 3 2 1

For the Birthday Club
You brought me to the table and back to life

CONTENTS

INTRODUCTION

"Hi, friend."

I first heard that greeting when I was home from college during an unexpected sabbatical. I found myself home, unenrolled, and rather alone. Most of my high school friends were on the normal college trajectory and away at school. And I, looking for something to do while I waited for my next stab at college life, got a job and made my first friend as a grown-up. At the time, it didn't feel like a monumental thing, but looking back I realize how special that was. Making new friends, outside of a familiar childhood environment like school or church, is a tricky thing. This first friend was a gift to me. At a time when I was not sure who I was or where I was going, she called me her friend.

"Friend!" she would announce joyously as she greeted me. I don't remember the first time I heard it, but I do remember my mom saying how much she loved that it was our way of greeting each other. It was more than a greeting, actually. It was a way of communicating belonging to each other, then and even now more than twenty years later. To be called a friend is an honor.

As we spend some time looking at how to navigate this tricky world of friendship, I want to start at the beginning. Wherever you find yourself right now in the realm of friendships—full to the brim, desperately lonely, or anywhere in between—there is a single friendship that, when pursued, will give you a place of belonging and comfort like no other, and that is the friendship of Jesus. There is no human relationship that can do for you what a friendship with him will do. As we look to him and the model he sets forth for friendship, I pray that if you have not experienced the personal friendship he offers to everyone, you get a glimpse of how good it is. What a friend we have in Jesus.

We are all built for community. Depending on your personality, this may be good news or perhaps not so good news. Community is experienced in many ways, friendship among them. In his book *The Search to Belong*, Joseph Myers brilliantly lays out four key aspects of community connection: public, social, personal, and intimate. Public is the largest space where we feel part of a larger group of people, such as at college, a larger church, or a great concert. Social is the space where we are interacting and connecting on a surface level with hundreds of people. This is most often experienced today in social media, but you can also find this sphere at your child's school, or maybe in a workplace or at a more traditional-sized church. Personal is the space of friendship. Here you interact with deeply with ten to twenty people, maybe less. You are known and seen. Intimate is the chosen few: a spouse, a best friend or two. Most people have one or two intimate connections in a lifetime.

Within our culture we excel at the public and social space. We find identity and community with large groups and are quite comfortable with surface-level interactions. Yet we are lonely. Over the past few years, major research institutes including CIGNA, Barna, and Brigham Young have all conducted research confirming the epidemic of loneliness. CIGNA, in particular, found that 54 percent of respondents said no one knows them. Using the standard tool for measuring loneliness, the UCLA loneliness scale, the average loneliness score in America is 44 (out of a scale of 20 to 80), thus categorizing the majority of Americans as lonely.

I believe the cause for this epidemic of loneliness is our neglect of the personal sphere of community. We are built to experience community at all the levels Myers listed, but a culture of public and social community with no personal community has left us lonely. Jesus himself confirms Myers's theory on the four spaces of community. Throughout the Gospels, we see Jesus creating and interacting with community in all four spaces. We see him feed the five thousand, gather at the temple, sit with the disciples, and focus on the three.

The only way to fight loneliness is to allow ourselves to be known. This doesn't happen at the surface level, so we must focus on our friendships. Jesus and the disciples walked this out, and we get to have a front-row seat as we observe and then replicate how to navigate the personal space well. As you will see, the richness of his example is breathtaking.

Let's follow Jesus and his friends.

CHAPTER ONE

MAKING FRIENDSHIP A PRIORITY

I used to be *so* good at friendship. I found joy in my friendships; they filled me up and I poured myself out in them. I loved being a good friend. Somewhere along the way of adulthood, motherhood, marriage, and life's ups, downs, and more downs, I lost my way. I had plenty of ladies in my life, yet I was missing the true enjoyment of friendship. My social calendar was full with coffee dates, playdates, volunteer meetings, and work events. I had more going on than the hours I could reasonably give to them. I found myself surrounded by people, but I was lonely and missing community.

What had gone wrong?

I had more people in my life than I could keep up with. I had a running list of ladies I wanted to connect with but didn't—and all the guilt that goes along with that. I had social media to show me all the parts of my friends' lives that I was missing (and the parties I wasn't invited to, either). I was full, stuffed actually, with social interactions, and yet I had no breathing room in my interactions. So why was my heart was crying out?

I was involved in a group for other moms and a small group from church, I had hundreds of friends on Facebook, and I knew all the moms at my kids' school. I would have wonderful conversations with all of these ladies. On paper, it looked as if I was doing all the things one is supposed to do to "find your tribe," and my calendar certainly had absolutely no space for any other endeavors. Yet there I was . . . frustrated, isolated, and firmly without "my people." The math wasn't adding up.

In what proved to be a rather brutal exercise, I set out to examine the current state of my friendships and community. Now, let's just take a moment and acknowledge how that sounds. I decided I had to work on friendship. Isn't friendship supposed to be easy? It sounds ridiculous that it was a year and a half of work in my life, but that is the truth because community building requires intentionality. If you want a deeper relationship with God, you have to spend time with God. If you want a deeper and more committed relationship with your husband, you have to spend time with him. It is the same for deep friendship. This feels countercultural to us, but we need to really push against the notion that friendship is easy or should just fall into place. We need to be intentional! There's no shame for where you are now, but this is the way to get to where you want to be, and I want you to join me here!

Here is what it boiled down to . . . I was spending more time (both physically and mentally) on friendlies and not nearly enough on friends. A "friendly" is what I call a person in your life who is more than an acquaintance but not a true, deep friend with whom you can share your heart. You may share pleasant chitchat with a friendly on the sideline of your child's soccer game, or start to realize you have things in common and even suggest that you get together. With busy schedules and chance meetings, you know it will likely never happen, but you at least attempt it.

Perhaps you share about a current struggle as you are awaiting pickup at school. "I would love to talk about this more," you both say (and truly mean), but there is no follow-up for either of you. Friendlies are the in-between. Some friendlies are "not yet friends," while others are considered "connected acquaintances." They aren't the ones you call when you run out of gas with a van full of kids, but more than likely you comment on pictures they post on Facebook or your kids go to school together.

Once you start to recognize a friendly, you will see there are lots of them in your life. Having friendlies in your life is not a bad thing. We need people in our lives, and we are called to be friendly to those we encounter. However, mistaking the plethora of friendlies in your life for deep friendship and community is a roadblock to cultivating a true community. We can come to believe the lie that this is what community actually looks like. For a season, I made that mistake. I thought because there were so many women I was interacting with that I was in community. In reality, I was just keeping myself busy and not investing deeply in anyone nor allowing them to invest deeply in me. As I settled into adulthood, I found myself settling for this pale substitute of connected, life-giving friendship. Basically, I had a built a life with lots of surface-level friendliness, and it left me feeling deflated. Community, real community, is made with intention and investment, and I was lacking both.

My "friendly" interactions had become the only interactions I was having. Even more, I had a reactionary position with all these women in my orbit. It felt like I was pouring out to whomever was in front of me with no thought of "Is this who I am called to invest in?" There was no intentionality, and the investment I did offer was, sadly, shallow and often short-lived. I was assuming that if someone was saying to me, "Let's have coffee" or "I would love to get the kids together," that they were my person, at least for the moment, and hopefully it would lead to a deeper connection.

In an effort to quench my thirst for depth, I was jumping about from one friendly to the next, attempting to create belonging and community with the hope of each friendly. And let me tell you, it was exhausting and unfulfilling! And here's the thing: surface-level relationships should not be exhausting to us. This happens when we have misplaced expectations on these friendlies in our lives. Friendlies aren't wrong, but if they are the only people you spend your time on, you will feel depleted because there is no commitment with friendlies—it's sometimes convenient and always casual.

So, as I was left with that nagging longing for community that friendlies were not filling, I would then fill up on interactions and information on social media. The challenge with social media interactions is that we mistake them for social interactions. While social media is not all bad, it will never replace face-to-face *relationships*. The two are, simply, unequal. One is built around a screen view, and the other is built around the entire view. When we consume a high volume of social media snippets and information, we fill our minds without gaining the positives of dwelling in authentic relationship. We use up our capacity to invest emotionally by wasting that precious resource on our friend's sister's cousin's wedding.

You know what I am talking about. . . . I see my friend tagged in a photo. . . . I click and before I know it, I have just spent ten minutes looking through a stranger's wedding album and comparing it to my current life. . . . And, wait, did I go to school with that girl on the dance floor? . . . And it looks like one of my son's classmates went to Disney . . . And look at that birthday event that

I didn't get invited to. . . . We click and we click and we ingest what does not satisfy us as we watch people's celebrations through the murky screen of a computer or phone and convince ourselves we have been filled up with social interactions.

In reality, we have just spent more minutes absorbing other people's lives without investing anything in the people who are actually around us. Comparison or jealousy often seeps in, which leads to feeling isolated, and we close off a part of our heart to a more genuine relationship than what we see with our eyes. Social media can offer some connection, it's true, but it is not the way to find community when we are lonely. We walk around with all of this surface-level knowledge of people's lives swirling in our brains, yet in our hearts we don't truly know them, and we are not known, either.

And that was me. I wasn't investing deeply or with intention and kept wondering why I was emotionally spent and still lonely. I got really honest about who I was interacting with and what those interactions looked like. Staring at a screen led to spending my capacity for empathy. A passing hello in the school hallway was not a friend about to be made if I never did anything about it. A calendar bursting at the seams left no room for intentional gatherings. The volume of interactions I had each day had no bearing on the quality of my community.

Have you ever stopped to realize how many people you interact with on a daily basis? It is quite astounding when you sit and think about it! It is so easy to feel tapped out on human interaction before ever connecting with a life-giving relationship. It is so easy to say yes to whomever happens to be in front of you without any forethought of community.

And that is the problem in a nutshell. Surrounded yet alone. Pouring out but not being filled up. Longing to be known.

Of course, our longing comes from an innate desire to be known by our Creator. There is no community or friendship that can substitute for a personal relationship with Jesus. Community is a gift from God, an experience in being known the way Jesus modeled as he was known by his Father. There was a deeper bond in God's purposes and plans for his Son, and there is for us as well in community. It's a way to bridge the gap and see Christ in the flesh and blood around us. Friendship—true, deep, abiding friendship—shaped by biblical example will fill us up in ways the friendlies never can.

I remember the first time I put words to this longing in my heart for deep, abundant friendship. At fourteen years old, I was at a sleepover with a newish friend. I had transferred to a new school the year before, and I spent that first year finding out what cliques did and didn't work for me. In a school of about two thousand kids, I had settled into a large group of friends that fit and felt right. By sophomore year I was no longer the new girl; I felt a part of the larger social dynamic, and yet something was missing. I was lacking a confidante, a friend that I could share with and count on in a deep way. That night of the sleepover, my newish friend and I were falling asleep talking about how hard it was, especially with girls, to find trustworthy friends. We took turns, almost finishing each other's sentences, sharing our heart cry. We deeply wanted to be known and trusted by a friend and to be that for someone else.

It was a very brave and bold conversation for two fourteen-year-old girls to have. It felt both vulnerable and safe. We both knew as we were sharing that the very thing we were missing had just been found in each other. I fell asleep that night relieved that I wasn't alone in my longing and hopeful that I had been given a glimpse of what true friendship could look like: brave, bold, honest, trusting, and trustworthy. After that sleepover, I was fully in the midst of a sweet season of friendship with my not-so-newish friend and others we brought into our circle. Naturally, there was the mix of teenage angst and drama, but looking back I realize that we did friendship well. I loved being a great friend, and I adored the wonderful friends I had. Yet somewhere along the way, in my early twenties and after, I lost the ability to be a great friend and to invest in the wonderful friends I had. Along the way of becoming a wife and mother and navigating the stresses of adult life, I lost my ability to find and nurture true friendship and genuine community.

So where did I lose my way?

I spent a lot of time feeding myself lies: My life is too busy for friendship. I have everything I need in my husband and kids. When life slows down, I will be better equipped to be a good friend. Yet the longing wouldn't leave. And my ability to handle life's challenges has often been the very reason I ended up feeling isolated. When many people face a crisis, their overwhelming need demands that others jump in. I now have learned that when I have a crisis, others sit back and watch because I haven't invited them in. I make sure things get done and handled with grace, tact, grit . . . whatever is necessary. A busy life becomes busier and more complicated, and most every challenge is met. However, I move too fast or get too busy, and no one recognizes that even though I am very capable, I still would love to have the company of friends alongside me. I build walls with my capability and make it almost impossible to get through.

Thankfully, I have learned that if I create the walls, I also need to show people how to enter. Sometimes that may look like opening a door in the wall and welcoming friends in, and sometimes that means tearing down the walls you built, trusting that your community is a safe place for you. I finally understood that waiting (and longing) for a friend to chip through my tough exterior was not the way to build friendships. It was as if I were sitting alone inside my walls, frustrated that no one was trying hard enough to get in. I wanted community, and I needed to make a clear path for others to get to know me, the real me. I was going to have to stand at the open door and say, "Come in, friends!" Deciding to invest in my community building was also a decision to tear down some walls. Boy, that was a tough one.

Maybe your roadblock looks nothing like mine. I have the roadblock of not allowing others in who want (and who I need) to be deeper connections. You may have been scarred from a past friendship hurt. The pain of betrayal causes many of us to stay isolated rather than attempt a deeper friendship again. If you have felt that hard loss of a friend or the deep wound from a trusted confidante's betrayal, you may wonder how you could ever open yourself up to that kind of potential hurt again. Perhaps you feel too hard to understand because your life is far more complicated or your past far darker than anyone would imagine. Or maybe you are simply content on your own and don't see the need to have others deeply rooted in your life. Whatever your reason, there is a yearning inside each one of us to be known and seen, and there is a God-designed community waiting for you. And it can be so much better together.

We are designed for community. It is written throughout Scripture that we are made to be part of something bigger, yet we fill our time with trivial and unfulfilling interactions and then wonder why we stay in the longing place.

There is a better way.

I knew I needed to make friendship a priority, so after intentional prayer and a few awkward emails, I met the new community around the table. The table has always been a place of joy and delight for me. All of my favorite things: gathering people, celebrating, serving. It all takes place at the table. When setting out on this friendship journey, I knew I needed to start there with people that God put on my heart to ask to join me.

Breaking bread, of course, requires a table not just to hold the elements but to center our hearts as well. The practice of coming together, sharing a meal, sharing time, and communing with one another is the essence of breaking bread together. But there is more. The richness and nuances of doing this, consistently, with people who matter to you, is where community building starts. There is a holy pause that comes from gathering: a moment when you look around the table at the faces of people who know you, truly know you, and love you just as you are, and you stop and breathe that in. You know that you are known. It happens at the table.

I really love the way *Urban Dictionary* defines "break bread": "to affirm trust, confidence, and comfort with an individual or group of people." Breaking bread is being known and celebrated and doing the same for others, and that requires a community. This is it! This is what our hearts long for, and not only is it a physical act; it brings physical gifts to us in the process!

At some point along the way, we have believed the lie that this type of community is an unattainable, idyllic anomaly. Communities gathering together, praying for each other, celebrating, living life together in a connected way is the stuff of movies, right? And if it does exist, that type of community works for some but wouldn't in our busy lives. How can we take on one more thing? Communities like that must be for people more put together, less busy, in a different stage than me. Unattainable and unsustainable, it feels like an impossible dream. Why else would we settle for anything less?

The truth is that this type of Breaking Bread Community *is* fully attainable, even in our actual, stuffed, overscheduled lives, if we open ourselves up to the invitation to come to the table. There is a requirement of intention and effort, to be sure. But it doesn't have to be perfect, and it doesn't have to be "when you are ready." We're already ready, so why are we waiting on a clean house or a clear schedule? As with all relationships, the way to a deeper place is spending more time together—this takes planning and commitment. But so do all the things we do for a family or someone you care for. So think of it as caring for *you* while you care for *them*.

It all begins with a vision of what this type of community can look like and an invitation to get started. For me, the invitation to gather with others at the table was the beginning of what has been the sweetest and most fulfilling season of my adulthood. I realized, as my community started to gather and celebrate and serve each other, that we were emulating another group of friends that gathered, celebrated, and served. How Christ gathered with his friends for that last meal has had a profound impact on the way I gather, interact with, and continue to nurture my community. I use the Last Supper as a model for what to emulate, how I interact with my friends, how I serve them and receive service, and how I handle conflict. I quite literally ask myself, "What did Jesus and the disciples do when they gathered?" and use the answers as my road map. Studying the Last Supper and the interactions of the disciples and Jesus has shown me the way to authentic and transformational friendships.

The world's most important dinner party is also a specific and replicable model of community lived out. Together we are going to examine the friendship community Christ shows us, his very own Breaking Bread Community, at the Last Supper.

MEET ME AT THE TABLE

We all know the story of the Last Supper. I bet when you picture the Last Supper, the image you see is pretty close to (if not exactly

like) da Vinci's painting of the same name. There is an assumed
understanding that we know the story and the people involved,
and we even have a collective (albeit perhaps inaccurate) visual
understanding of the Upper Room based on this famous work of
art. But there is so much depth packed into this singular evening
that we have barely scratched the surface!

I love research, reading, and studying things that I want to
know more about. I love God's Word and diving deep into it to
better understand and appreciate the majesty of the Bible. I also
am a fast reader and skim often. The challenge found in studying
such a familiar text is that it becomes very easy to skim. We are
going to push back hard against this inclination together. When
we move slowly through a text and savor each word, we are able to
see deeper and more complex meaning in what was once familiar.
We find the amazing in the already known.

The richness of all that transpired at the Last Supper warrants
such a closer look to fully understand friendship and how we are
to live in it like Jesus did. Christ's last meal, the one he chose to
spend with his friends, gives us a front-row seat to what living out
friendship looks like in the way Christ calls us live. We get to be
"flies on the wall" and are able to watch and learn how this group of
friends interacted, what they were taught as a way to nurture their
friendships, why they gathered and under what circumstances . . .
every moment of the Last Supper has implications for our community building today.

We have been exhausting ourselves trying to conjure up community and abolish our loneliness in all the wrong ways. It turns
out that the Last Supper is not just a beautiful picture of community. It is an actual road map showing us how to nurture a Breaking
Bread Community in our own lives! The Last Supper gives us a
reason to hope with others, a way to celebrate with joy, and the

gift of experiencing something that is often hard to put into words. This kind of community is surely needed and wanted in our culture today.

As we spend time dwelling in the text, I challenge us to notice all the interactions during the evening of the Last Supper. Through the accounts in the four Gospels (Matthew, Mark, Luke, and John), we have the ability to be in the room with this community as they are called to gather, celebrate, learn, and serve together. We see Christ offer some of his most powerful teaching, not to the masses but to his community. We see how friends deal with betrayal, hurt feelings, and hard times. We see how to face great disappointment and loss.

The Last Supper was the most important gathering of friends that has ever taken place. At this final gathering of his disciples, Christ demonstrated what friendship can be. The beauty, nuance, power, and example of the Last Supper has been an inspiration to me in the years I have studied it. It is rich beyond measure, and I fear that we are missing a lot of its majesty. We are going to spend time studying the Last Supper, and there, I believe, we will see what we are called to live out as friends in community. Friendship shaped by this example will also be a world-changer for us, a symphony of feasting and loving that requires our giving and our partaking.

While a study of this most incredible night will take us through all of the Gospel accounts (Matt. 26:17–35; Mark 14:12–31; Luke 22:7–38; and John 13:1–17:26) of the Last Supper, we will start by reading one account in full and looking at how we can follow in our friendships. Let's start looking for the road map that shows us the way to find and live within our own Breaking Bread Community.

We will begin with Luke for our overview of the scriptures. Read the account in Luke 22:7–38 and keep in mind what we have talked about in this chapter. Read slowly and picture Christ gathering his community to celebrate and share some earth-shattering news. When reading Scripture, it is important to remember that these were real people, real friends. Notice the humanness and relationships so beautifully on display.

As you read through the account in Luke (as well as the other Gospels), it is apparent that friendship and community are more than one-on-one relationships. In Jesus and the disciples, we see a group of friends. Groups can be intimidating and daunting. The personalities, the schedules, the varied backgrounds—there is a lot to complicate things. Often, our response is to focus on friendships in much more manageable sizes. Within a community of friends, there are, by nature and necessity, individual relationships. But these should not be confused as only singular friendships. A singular friendship is a friendship that exists within its own one-on-one environment. Singular friendships aren't bad relationships to have, but they shouldn't be the only way we to experience friendship. When we limit our definition of friendship to one-on-one relationships, we limit the richness and fullness of what friendship is designed to be. I think for most, myself included, one-on-one friendships can be much easier to imagine. While all the lessons we learn through the Last Supper can certainly be applied to one-on-one friendships, the bigger challenge for us all is to step into a community of friendships like we see on display that night. As we begin this journey of watching Christ and his friends—as we watch them break bread together—may we, too, be spurred on to experience the fullness of friendship.

BREAK BREAD TOGETHER

After studying God's Word, we will spend time reflecting, praying, and taking action. Let's have our friendships transformed by our time in the Word!

1. List out your fears about stepping into deep community. Really write them down! When we name a fear, we are better prepared to speak to it.

2. How much of your time is being spent on friendlies and social media? What kind of fulfillment are you finding there? What is one change you can make to how you are investing in social media or friendlies that will create space for your community to flourish?

3. What is your ideal image of community, and how much of that do you see reflected in the Last Supper?

4. Write out a description of what you see at the Last Supper . . . the beginning of your road map.

Pray with me for God's direction in your friendships.

> *Father,*
>
> *We know our longing to be known comes from our innate desire to be known by you. Be with us as we dive deep into your Word and seek your will in our lives. Direct us, Lord, as we seek our own Breaking Bread Community. Help us face the fears we have about being known by others and grant us discernment as we examine how we spend our time and who we invest in. Help us to fully step into the Upper Room and see what deep, abiding community looks like as we seek the same in our lives. Bring us closer to Jesus and guide us, Lord, we pray. Amen.*

We are lost and lonely. And, of course, the answer can be found in Jesus Christ. Come, let's break bread together.

CHAPTER TWO

EXCLUSIVITY AND DIVERSITY

As a typical firstborn, type A, enneagram 8, I set out to solve my friendship problem (or lack thereof!) and committed to making it a priority. Looking at the abundance of people in my life that I was already interacting with, I quickly became overwhelmed. I was surrounded by so many people! I think this is a huge challenge for women. We are surrounded, but are we invested? We perceive our friendship needs as being met based on how many social interactions we have on any given day. And even if we are aware that our more profound community needs aren't being met, we certainly have been spent by the plethora of our interactions. Therefore, we have nothing left to give to relationships that go deeper.

I realized that I wasn't engaging in authentic community. I wasn't being thoughtful about who I was investing in and certainly not prayerful about it. This is not how community is designed to be. The type of community we are after is found in knowing others deeply and being fully known ourselves. It's in a life-giving context of both giving and receiving. Often, our short interactions with people are mostly about what we can give to appear amiable. But there is the exchange between giving *and* receiving. I realized I could not get this from social media or a life filled with only friendlies.

The conclusion I came to was that I was going to have to invest in "my people," whoever "they" were. As women we are inundated with messages such as "find your tribe," "love your people," "#squad-goals," and so on. And to be honest, none of them sat very well with me. This type of thinking always led me to feel like an outsider. I didn't know who my people were anymore! I saw groups of ladies gathering together on social media or on TV, and it was as if these "squads" had magically found each other and instant community.

I attempted to replicate what I thought I was seeing and was left lonelier than before. I invested in whomever was in front of me, regardless of whether they were really the people with whom I was called to build friendships. I found myself dreading time with these people instead of looking forward to our time together, because it was born out of obligation and misplaced expectations. I tried to squeeze my way into long-established groups of friends yet maintained my position as an outsider by not fully investing in anyone.

I had exhausted myself trying to find community my way, and I didn't end up with anything transformative. What if finding my tribe wasn't my job at all? What if my job was to ask the One who created the original Breaking Bread Community who my community was? That seemed like a much better start than I had previously tried.

After this realization, I knew where to begin: prayer. I prayed fervently that I would know who to invest in and which people God wanted in my life at a deeper level. This changed everything.

I began to pray, specifically, for God to bring to mind the women he wanted me to dwell in community with. The burden was no longer on me to "find my people." As I prayed and waited, I was so surprised at the short list of names I was given. It looked as though God was keeping my community small, and I wasn't sure how I felt about that.

My perception had always been that Christians welcome everyone, we keep the door open, we invite all the people all the time, and we serve everyone. I love this about being a Christian, but here's the thing . . . I had twisted that idea in my head to mean that I needed to be all-inclusive *all* the time. But then I realized that the same Jesus who had swarms of people around him, who fed the five thousand, who walked among the throngs of hundreds of people also had a small group that was his closest circle. There is room, and more importantly a strong example, for *both* enjoying the throngs and the select few.

EXCLUSIVITY

The notion of exclusivity can be hard to accept. Having been left out of things myself, I know it is hard to be on that side of the equation. But community, as demonstrated by Jesus and the disciples, is not for everyone you serve, know, or even love. The abundance of community is found in going deep with a few. As a generation, we run the risk of missing out on that abundance found in deep-rooted community. If we do not accept exclusivity, we can spend our whole lives including everybody and knowing nobody. God has a handful of women ready to bless us with, and we're going to miss it having superficial coffee talk with one hundred friendlies, rather than transformative fellowship with the few. If we shy away from exclusivity, we will miss the fullness of life-giving friendship.

Think of it in terms of a party and how the quality of interactions varies depending on the guest count. There was a time when our family had some amazing Christmas open houses. Year after year we would open our home for about six hours on a Saturday in December, and we welcomed everyone. It was a beautiful time of about a hundred neighbors, family, friends—old and new—all mingling and celebrating the magic of the Christmas season. It was festive and fun and frantic. The beauty of seeing all these people gathering and interacting and experiencing the hospitality of Jesus was something very special. A few years in, our family was in desperate need of a slow season, so we skipped the open house and instead hosted a series of much, *much* smaller get-togethers. Those celebrations were sweet and focused, with more eye contact and time to linger in conversation. The interactions, while involving fewer people, were richer. The abundance of the big party cannot replace the abundance found in meaningful interactions. This is the same with nurturing a community.

We must embrace this notion of exclusivity because we simply do not have the time or emotional availability to go deep with all the women in our life. We have a need for depth, and the disconnect between what we have capacity-wise and what we need is where we sit in that longing place. We can bridge that gap by going deep with a few—something our busy lives can handle and our hearts are crying out for! We are called to go deep (being in more personal community) and wide (being open to many). But we can't keep going wider in an attempt to compensate for lack of depth. Jesus shows us that sometimes the table is small, and that is exactly as it is designed to be to experience rich, abundant community.

The exclusivity of deep friendship does not prevent us from investing in others outside the inner circle. Digging deep with a handful of women actually enables us to serve the many. We *get* to do both. It's just that at one level we can only invest a certain amount of time, and the other level gives us the freedom (not pressure) to spend more time. It becomes like the way we prioritize time with family. When we have a clearer view on the ones we get to invite into deep community, we have healthier relationships all around. I learned how to be a good friend again by focusing on the few, and that allowed me to be a better friend to many. How? Because it wasn't as important that everyone know me. I was free to show everyone that I noticed them.

Once I focused on cultivating community among a handful of women (six, to be exact!), I was filled up. With my needs being met and also the opportunity to pour myself out to serve others, I had so much more to give in my other interactions. The friends and friendlies in my life were no longer taxing. What once felt burdensome, I now saw with fresh eyes. The friends and friendlies no longer represented failure or disappointment. Instead, these women represented simple, sweet interactions throughout the day. I was able to enjoy those relationships for exactly what they were. I greeted women that I passed in the school hallways with genuine greetings rather than a guilty wave, knowing I never made time for the get-together I had suggested.

Accepting exclusivity within my Breaking Bread Community allowed me to adjust the expectations I had for the other women, friends and friendlies, in my life. It wasn't until my need to have this type of community was met that I even realized all the guilt and displaced expectations I had wrapped up in these other relationships.

I have friendships that used to be a daily thing, and now, due to the simple progression of time and families, they are a yearly thing. For a long time as the friendship went through this natural progression, I struggled. I experienced anger, annoyance, rejection, and disappointment, and I probably caused others to feel the same. My expectations of the friendships were not in line with reality. Nothing had gone wrong with our relationship; it was just shifting as our lives shifted. Once I focused on the people God invited me to focus on, everything changed. There was an easing of the pressure. Our yearly meet-up became one of joy rather than one of wishing for something more. When you're digging deep with the right people at the right time, the rest works itself out. It's easy to offer grace and appreciate the women in your life for who they are if you're not forcing the kind of community, a Breaking Bread Community, where it does not fit.

Similarly, I was able to embrace the sweet long-distance friendships I had with college roommates and high school classmates. I have a group of friends from high school—amazing women—and we all lost a parent when we were pregnant with our first child. I know, it's shocking. We were tight in high school, and then this crazy series of events cemented a sisterhood that we never would have predicted. I love these women deeply. They understand the things that happen to you upon losing a parent at such a tender time. We don't all live within the same town, or even in the same state. They have a unique role in my life, and when I recognized that this unique role was what we were called to play in each other's lives, I also realized this group does not replace my need for a close community in my everyday life.

Once I understood the call to a Breaking Bread Community, it lessened a burden I had put on these other relationships. My expectations were realigned in a way that honored the bond of friendship we share; I accepted the physical distance between us, and the rapid-fire yearly catchups once felt to be so much less than our friendship deserved became ample. I found myself in a place of gratitude that these amazing women know my history and have a piece of my heart, yet feeling peace that they are not involved in my everyday comings and goings. No guilt, no regret, no animosity.

I used to think that friendships like this—long-lasting, inherently special, yet not part of my everyday life—were enough to sustain my need for friendship. And that's just not so. I wasn't honoring these friendships with my unrealistic expectations. I wanted more than I could get or give and was wasting time bemoaning what wasn't available in those relationships. I also feared that diving deep with a new community would somehow dishonor these women who matter so much to me. I was, yet again, missing the mark. As a completely unexpected blessing, accepting exclusivity within my Breaking Bread Community actually made me a better friend across the board. I felt freedom to dive deep with women God himself invited into my life, and freedom to accept these longtime friendships for exactly what they were!

DIVERSITY

You may be surprised who God invites into your life. The handful of women with whom I started this journey are a unique mix. Some are women I had known for almost a decade and always thought I would like to spend more time with but never stepped in. Some are women I knew peripherally and had never bothered to truly get to know. And others are women I had started to go deeper with after having served together, or women I barely knew, but clearly God had called us together. The bottom line is that I stopped acting as if I knew who would serve me best, and who I would serve best, and instead decided to listen and obey God as I asked him to show me who to initiate this type of Breaking Bread Community with. This small group of women was the beginning of my reclaiming community and more rooted friendships. Just as he pulled the disciples together, God pulled us together, and I am so thankful he did.

The men who made up the twelve were so varied that it is shocking to think this group was designed to flourish together! Within the group, we find optimists and pessimists. We find scholars and fishermen and the lowest of the low, a tax collector. We find those known for their hatred and zeal, as well as those known for their love and forgiveness. We find the doubter and the one anxious for honor. We find intense Jewish nationalists as well as disciples of John the Baptist. This group with seemingly little in common was called to gather and fellowship together. The differences among them seem to be the one thing the group has in common.

When we see Jesus and the twelve at the table, we see that our friends are going to be diverse. The diversity of the disciples is a beautiful and unexpected thing. With complete intention, Jesus gathered a mix of outcasts and unlikely friends to walk together with him. They were fishermen and tax collectors, pacifists and zealots, men that had no business being unified. But God had a plan.

What seems illogical to us makes perfect sense when we consider Jesus. He reflects the kingdom fully and therefore in many different ways. While I am able to reflect Jesus this side of heaven, I am limited in how that manifests itself. The same can be said for you. To fully reflect the fullness of who Jesus is, we need each other and friends who are different from us. When we come together with a group of diverse people, we more closely reflect the dynamic goodness and fullness of God. So it makes sense that friendships designed to reflect Christ must contain a dynamic and diverse group of people.

The group of women I found gathered around my table is reflective of God's kingdom, and that means we are a diverse group. The diversity found in the kingdom is such a beautiful gift. These God-designed communities we are yearning for will, of course, reflect the same diversity. This can be uncomfortable, as we tend to draw near to those we are most similar to. But when we ask God to do this work, we must trust him to gather the women. After all, the burden of finding your tribe is not one you want!

When preparing for this diverse group to gather, we remember that diversity is more than outward appearances. Diversity will be present in many ways within your Breaking Bread Community. In my community, we have many different backgrounds and upbringings represented; we have different schooling philosophies represented; we have those who love to camp and those who prefer to travel the luxury route. These differences may seem inconsequential, but as you begin to do life together, you will see the ways God uses these differences to challenge you, encourage you, and expand your horizons. It is, just as his kingdom is, beautiful.

MEET ME AT THE TABLE

Jesus was sitting down for what he knew would be the last meal of his earthly life. It was the Passover that would acknowledge him as Messiah. There could not be a more important celebration.

> When it was evening, he reclined at table with the twelve. (Matt. 26:20 ESV)

Jesus could have invited anyone to this meal, and he invited the twelve. He didn't invite the powerful or influential; he invited the handful he had been in deepest community with. The Last Supper, to me, is one of the coolest things Jesus did during his ministry on earth. He wanted to leave the world with the last and the best of his teachings. He needed to explain his death and the fact that the entire world was about to be turned upside down. And how did he do it? He brought his closest friends together. It is so easy to miss, the exclusivity and the diversity of the twelve.

When we see Jesus and the twelve at the table, we see that we are made for community, and at the same time we are not intended to be in intimate, deep community with everyone. This is why God's calling for the people in your life is so important. The intimacy required in living out this kind of friendship requires a trust and faith that is found in the confidence of answered prayer that he brought you together. Knowing that God has his hand in the choosing of your friends changes everything. You can step into intimacy and serving with comfort, assurance, and discernment, all because you started with prayer.

As Jesus was approaching his death, he did what so many of us have done when facing the unimaginable: he circled the wagons. If you have had to face a crisis, and I have yet to meet someone who hasn't, then you can relate. There is a sense that the first step is to draw close those who are in the inner circle. I am not advocating shutting yourself off—Christ himself clearly didn't do that. But when facing the unimaginable, it is natural and good to sit with those in your closest community first.

I have a tendency to overcomplicate things. This is seen most clearly when I start working on a guest list. I have an uncanny ability to take something as simple as a playdate and turn it into a study in interpersonal dynamics. It escalates quickly into a series of if-then statements that inevitably results in a guest list triple the original size. If I invite this one, then I have to invite these two as well, and so on, until my playdate of six is at least twenty people. What started out as an exercise in hospitality erupts into an exercise of inclusion to the nth degree.

But when faced with crisis events, when we celebrated what we knew would be Mom's last Christmas, when we were in the hospital for days or weeks on end, when we had devastating news to share—at those times and during others like them, it was crystal clear who was supposed to be there. The people who knew us best, the friends who were not scared off by the chemo and radiation, by the brain trauma, the ones who knew our history, our nuances, who could speak to us as only those who know you intimately can. They are the ones we *craved* to be with. And we knew they felt compelled to be with us—they wanted to stand in the storm with us.

But it only works if you already know who your people are. I am not suggesting that Jesus faced the Last Supper (or his death) as if it were a crisis. In fact, he did just the opposite. But the act of circling the wagons is one that we can relate to. There are times when it is right and necessary to keep the circle tight. Prior to the Last Supper, the disciples had lived out friendship. They had already stepped into community with each other so that when Jesus called them together for that most important celebration, they were ready, together.

Friends matter to God. Your friends matter to God. And when asked, he will provide the most amazing, unique, diverse, challenging group of friends to walk with you. Not what you pictured? Join the club! I wasted a lot of time believing that I knew who my friends were supposed to be.

I really don't like being told what I will like. In the past, the joke was if you wanted me to try a restaurant, you shouldn't tell me how much I was going to like it. My pride stepped in and created a barrier to the notion that I could be predictable or similar to someone else, and I would likely not set foot in said restaurant. It's not pretty. This prideful stubbornness is something that is constantly being refined in me. I wasn't even aware of this tendency until I began being intentional about my friends.

I never considered myself to be set in my ways about my friends, but it was true. I had heard for years that I would just love this girl Jen. Mutual friends suggested over and over again that we would really get along. Well, knowing how I react to restaurant recommendations, you can imagine how well *that* went over. The only reason I avoided her friendship was my pride in thinking I knew who my friends were going to be. We are polar opposites in many ways: she is gentle and I am harsh; she is laid-back and I am *not*; she is a vegetarian and I love steak; she is yin and I am yang; and it all seemed like way too much of a stretch to form a friendship.

It wasn't until I prayed specifically for God to show me who he wanted in my life that I reached out. Because you guessed it, Jen was at the top of the list. I stepped into friendship with her, and let me tell you I have never had a friend bless me so much and so specifically simply by being herself. I thank God for her and for her friendship in my life. I am a better person and a better friend for having Jen walk with me. God knows who I need and who needs me. He knows who you need as well, and you can bet it isn't going to be the list of friends you would make on your own. His version of friendship is so much richer and more abundant than we can imagine ourselves.

I am so thankful that Jesus invited the twelve to dinner that night. It was a night that changed history, and while doing that, it also laid out how to have God-sized friendship and community. It starts with exclusivity and diversity.

BREAK BREAD TOGETHER

After studying God's Word, we will spend time reflecting, praying, and preparing to take action. Let's have our friendships transformed by our time in the Word!

1. Do you have an initial discomfort at the notion of exclusivity? What are your concerns about exclusivity? What truths can you tell yourself to speak to those fears or concerns?

2. List out preconceptions you have about who your friends should be. Do you have these types of diverse friends in your life?

3. Remember a time when you were blessed with an unlikely friendship.

4. To whom do you draw close naturally? Do you have diverse friends in your life? Challenge yourself to be open to community with unlikely friendships.

5. Write down the names of friends God is calling you to go deeper with.

Father,

We thank you for how you made our world—diverse and varied—and we pray for communities that are the same. And yet we know that we are also called to small tables sometimes, deeper relationship with a few rather than the throngs. Help us to see how the two work together. Help us to know who is in our Breaking Bread Community. Lord, bring names to our minds. Help us to set aside any expectations of what our community should look like, and knit us closer to the ones you are calling us to live in community with. Amen.

CHAPTER THREE

WILL YOU BE MY FRIEND?

When my family moved around the time I was graduating eighth grade, we ended up getting a house in a new school district. Our home was right on the edge of the neighboring school district, but yes, it was over the border placing me firmly in a new group of students and teachers. The only person I even knew in that district was my friend's dad, who was a guidance counselor in the high school. I did not know a single student. And yet, starting at a new high school full of twenty-five hundred strangers was not a particularly nerve-wracking venture for me. I was a smart, confident, and self-assured girl.

The first day of school arrived and I was ready. I enjoyed my classes, navigated the building with ease, and felt great. However, all confidence flew out the window at the end of fourth period because next was . . . lunch. Who would I sit with? Would I have to approach people and ask to sit with them? Or worse yet, would I be the only person eating alone? The fear of rejection and embarrassment was swirling inside me. I stood frozen in the doorway of the massive cafeteria, unable to step inside. I retreated to a bench under the stairs and watched all the people, the friendships, awaiting me if I could just get myself to walk through that door.

If we are being honest, isn't that where we often still land? Fear of rejection and embarrassment keeps us frozen in place rather than moving forward—into the cafeteria then and into true community now. Everyone feels nervous when preparing to step into a Breaking Bread Community. Approaching a new friend or suggesting that we invest deeper into an already existing friendship is nerve-wracking. The awkwardness or apprehension can often intimidate us, causing us to miss out.

But the only way to get from where we are to where we want to be is by inviting others in. So, deep breath. We are going to do this together.

We begin with prayer. Seeking God's desire for community in our lives is paramount. Of all the mistakes I have made over the years in seeking community, leaving this step out has been by far the most damaging. When we start with prayer, we end up with an assurance that, in fact, God has been the one to design and create the community we invest in and are a part of.

The assurance that comes from prayer is, as my pastor calls it, joyful certainty. We get to have that certainty because Jesus himself tells us, "Whatever you ask in my name, this I will do, that the Father may be glorified in the Son. If you ask me anything in my name, I will do it" (John 14:13–14 ESV). So, let's ask him. Let's be bold with our prayers and ask Jesus to put the women whom he has called into our lives foremost in our minds. Let's align our desires with his through prayer and ask him to show us whom to break bread with as we step into community.

Of course, this is a process, and it will take different amounts of time for each of us. As we start to pay attention to those around us and ask God, "Is that her?," we will gain clarity as to whom to invite into community with us. As we learned in Chapter Two, we are going to set aside any notions we have about who these people may be and instead listen. I believe so strongly that God has women at the ready for you. If we want God-designed communities, we must check and see who he has designed for us.

As I began to pray over my friendship problem and the direction God wanted me to take, names starting coming to me, and yes, they were a varied group. As I spent several weeks imagining and praying over this would-be community, the Lord began working on me and my heart. In the waiting, while I was praying for women to be made known to me, he shifted my idea of who my community would be composed of and opened my eyes to the reality that they would be different ladies than I had assumed they would be. He helped me work through some feelings of uncertainty as the names he brought forth started to settle into my heart. One by one, a handful of names came to me.

The concept of checking in with God before diving into friendships can be applied whether you are seeking a whole community or perhaps feeling a desire to go deeper with a particular person. Oftentimes you meet a person and seem to have an instant connection with her. Maybe you have a lot in common, maybe you have struck up an internet friendship, maybe you keep running into her at events and realize, "Oh! I think we are supposed to be friends." Before you go there, stop and pray. Literally ask God if this is a friendship to pursue. He will let you know. Praying for that clarity before you dive in will help give you confidence as you invest your time and your emotions.

This is a practice we see Jesus himself demonstrate for us in Luke 6:12–16. The night before he selected the twelve, he prepared himself through prayer. Scripture says he spent the night praying to God. The next morning, he called the twelve from among the followers to be designated as his apostles, his constant companions, commissioned by Christ himself. First, he prayed.

I have chased after friendships that were, in hindsight, not the ones designed for me. It is exhausting and stressful. It can feel like pushing a square peg into a round hole. When things don't fit, when you keep asking for meet-ups and the answer is no or indifference, when it never quite comes together and you are left with the dreaded feeling of wondering what's wrong with you, perhaps you too are chasing friendships not designed for you. I have found that adopting the simple practice of checking in before you dive in to be tremendously helpful. Having walked through this season of feeling lonely and out of place, I realized I had *never* asked God who he had chosen for my friendships. And now, on the other side of it, I realize how much better it is to have that knowledge on the front end of the friendship.

As for my community, once I had the handful of ladies clear, I took a deep breath and sent out what felt like the most vulnerable email I had ever sent. The email was short and sweet. It simply said, "I would like to spend more time with you and want to do so in an intentional way. Are you in?" Basically I passed a note (like we used to do in school before the age of texting) and asked, "Will you be my friend?" I'm not suggesting an email is necessary. You may be far braver than me and actually have the nerve to discuss this in person or on a phone call, like grown-ups do. But I *am* asserting that an invite of some kind is mandatory.

Why can't we just fall into sweet friendships? Why does it involve an awkward moment at the beginning? Here's why: we don't want to waste time, ours or theirs. When we haven't been clear, there can be so much miscommunication and missed expectations. There may be people you want to invest in, but they simply don't have the resources to reciprocate. There is real clarity found in the invitation, and that clarity is a huge gift.

So let's get over our fears and just ask! When diving into a new friendship that will lead to the kind of impactful community we are after, we want to start with clear intentions and expectations. So we ask, "Do you want to invest in a friendship?" Through the next chapter, we will discuss what this investing can look like. For now, I want to focus on pushing past the fear of rejection or embarrassment and just go for it. Extend the invite.

About two years ago, we decided to begin homeschooling. The decision was a long time coming, and as it happens, we were making the decision at the same time another friend, Reneé, was doing the same. As we gathered together over coffee with our dear friend Jen who is also a homeschooler, to share what we were planning for the upcoming school year, we began dreaming aloud of what it might look like to homeschool. Ideas began to be shared, and there were quite a few tentative moments of "maybe we could" or "it might be nice if." Basically, we were all dancing around the issue of doing this together or simply simultaneously. The question ultimately was: Would we be doing this in community together?

And then Reneé had the courage to say it: "Would you like to do this together?" The invite. That one brave sentence made such a difference in how we moved forward. "*Yes!*" was the immediate and enthusiastic answer. Because we were invited into community, I knew our place. I knew who was ready to pray with me through this next chapter in very specific ways. I knew who we would be investing in with time and care because there was already a commitment. The invite made all the difference. We knew that when we were bouncing ideas of field trips off each other, there was a sweet solidarity because we had made an intentional choice. As the one receiving the invite, I knew where we stood and then had the freedom to move forward with joyful certainty.

Assuming you will be the one extending the invite, remember you have the specific assurance that comes from having prayed and waited on the Lord to light the way. None of this is ours to design or manage. When God nudges me toward a new friend or a deeper relationship with someone currently in my orbit, I want to honor him by honoring the nudge and extending the invite.

Back to my original invitation. . . . The downside of sending an email, versus having a conversation, is that I had to wait for the response. As soon as I hit send, I wanted to crawl under the table and hide. I was at once relieved and terrified. As I waited for the responses, I was continually reminding myself that I had the assurance that God designed the community I was seeking. As you will see, I didn't have to wait long, and that is a sign that I was on the right path. The first response came back. It was from the person I knew the least and was the most nervous about, and the answer was a resounding and enthusiastic yes! With that first reply, I exhaled and sat back, amazed at what God was already doing. All the ladies I reached out to were equally excited, and here was the part that surprised me: they were yearning for connectedness as well!

This same idea can be applied to friends who already exist in your life where there is a desire for more. Remember my friend Reneé? We had known each other for almost ten years when she extended an invite. We had seasons of interacting more and seasons of interacting less. The only thing that ultimately changed that dynamic was her invitation. She prayerfully invited me to enter into community with her, and I am so thankful she did.

Today, after the invitation, I can say we are knitted together in a very specific way, and that was all made possible by her invitation.

By the time Reneé and I connected over homeschooling, I had been in the practice of prayerfully extending and accepting invitations for a while. I was able to respond with certainty because I had become attuned to my soul cry for the right community. When you are in the habit of praying and checking in with the Spirit, you begin to cultivate an almost immediate sense of which invite is for you.

MEET ME AT THE TABLE

Stepping away from the Last Supper for a moment, we need to see how this community came together in the first place.

> As Jesus was walking beside the Sea of Galilee, he saw two brothers, Simon called Peter and his brother Andrew. They were casting a net into the lake, for they were fishermen. "Come, follow me," Jesus said, "and I will send you out to fish for people." At once they left their nets and followed him.
>
> Going on from there, he saw two other brothers, James son of Zebedee and his brother John. They were in a boat with their father Zebedee, preparing their nets. Jesus called them, and immediately they left the boat and their father and followed him. (Matt. 4:18–22)

Here in Matthew, we are able to listen to that exact moment when Jesus extended the invitation into community to Peter and Andrew and then James and John. Here is what I see when we look closely at the Scripture: clear and concise invitations, boldness, and immediate response.

Have you ever been extra wordy out of nervousness? I sure have! My natural inclination is to use ten words when three will do. Add in nerves or fear of rejection, and I can easily outtalk the best of them. As we look to Jesus to see how he invited community together, we see the opposite happening. Jesus's brevity as he invited Peter into community with him is almost shocking. "Follow me" is so simple, and yet it does cut to the point. Let this be our friendly reminder that we do not need to overcomplicate our invitation. There is no need to perseverate on the perfect words or the perfect way to extend the invite. Let's instead let the words be fewer but the intention be greater.

We have freedom to offer our invitation into community in a similar manner, simple and straightforward. As you prepare to invite others, challenge yourself to keep it short and sweet, trusting the Spirit will be doing the heavy lifting for you to communicate in a way perhaps you couldn't anticipate. Also notice there was no hesitation when Jesus extended his invitation. The boldness that Jesus displayed is grounded in the same assurance we have. Assurance that we are pursuing a God-designed community. I know this has been said already, but this is where prayer becomes paramount. Assurance comes when you fully recognize that God himself is working this out for you.

And my favorite part—the immediacy of response. We see the word *immediate* used in both encounters here. Immediacy is a good sign that you are walking with the Spirit. You can anticipate an immediate response from those who are designed to be in community with you. And that is real. I went back and looked at the time stamps on that first email thread, and there was a one-minute gap between my send and the first reply. Immediacy comes because the women we are inviting in are yearning as well. Remember this as you extend the invite. The invitation into community may be offering them something they deeply need. I was so self-focused at that time, so keenly aware of what I was lacking in my life, that I was taken aback by how deeply the invitation resonated with my friends.

We are also called to leave some things behind. In Matthew 4:22, we see James and John leave not just their boat (their livelihood) but also their father. They left what they knew as they set out on the adventure of joining in this community. Part of stepping into community for us will also require our leaving some things behind. For us, it will look like leaving behind our notions of the familiar. Perhaps it will look like leaving behind our notions of isolation or independence. Take heart—you too are about to start an amazing adventure.

BREAK BREAD TOGETHER

After studying God's Word, we will spend time reflecting, praying, and preparing to take action. Let's have our friendships transformed by our time in the Word.

1. Pray specifically for direction and confirmation from God about who you should invite into community.

2. Pay attention to the stirring of your spirit as you are led to your community.

3. Prepare to invite. You can practice this first!

4. Extend an invitation. This can be to several at once or one friend at a time as they are brought to mind.

Lord,

We are first and foremost thankful for the invitation you extend to all of us to join you in relationship. You are a God of friendships and community, and we are people yearning for that very thing. As we seek the people we will invest in, Lord, we pray for your intercession. Bring the people you desire for our community to us. Father, show us the way to our people and then grant us the boldness to invite them in. Lord, we pray for the leaping of their spirit at the invitation as we begin this great adventure together. Amen, indeed.

CHAPTER FOUR

PREPARE WELL

I remember the first time I heard about a birthday club. I was working, setting up a wedding, and one of the floral assistants told me she had to leave by three that afternoon because she had Birthday Club, and she simply couldn't miss it. I could tell this gathering was important. As we worked throughout the afternoon, I asked her to tell me more about this club of hers. What I assumed was a complicated endeavor was actually quite simple. The Birthday Club, a group of ladies who had made a pact to celebrate each other's birthdays, had two ingredients that made it an easy yes: rhythms and reliability. The "birthday girl" would pick the day, time, and location of her celebration, and it was up to everyone else to give their best effort to attend. I can still see her face beaming as she shared about her beloved club, and I could tell that I was being let in on a great treasure. My heart leapt as she described her sweet gatherings with a mix of ladies all gathered together to celebrate one another because, really, how great does it sound?

"Great idea," I thought, as I stood there yearning to have friends to celebrate with me in the way she was describing. That thought was followed swiftly by the caveat "not for now." I told myself my life was far too busy, and I had far too little time to invest in something like that. Too much preparation required. The irony of the event planner being too busy to plan an event for herself was not lost on me, and I filed away the idea. I told myself that at some point I would have room for community, room in my calendar and in my life to gather and celebrate. I was buying into the lie that I was too busy to do this type of gathering now, not later. Have you ever felt that way? This whole concept of deep community is lovely, but how could I ever make it work with my crazy, busy schedule? I am going to tell you something I wish I had told myself in that moment. "Too busy" is a lie.

Fast-forward to the realization that community building and friendship *was* worthy of my attention and intention, my preparation. I was still left with the struggle of legitimately making time to invest in deep friendship. No shocker—eight years after I had first heard of a birthday club, my calendar was even more full than before! Gathering together with friends as a way to foster community was going to take *time*. Even further, it would require holding time for this purpose, and that would require preparation. Holding space on your calendar to invest in your community is a valuable undertaking. We struggle with overpacked schedules as it is, while simultaneously being bombarded with messages to hold margin. How do you justify devoting hours in your day to building community?

There was a time when my calendar was a brilliantly planned yet impossible puzzle that was scheduled to the minute. What looked lovely on paper was also totally unattainable with no breathing room. Even worse, the important was given no more value than the mundane. I felt a need to fill every moment. There was no room for things to go wrong without causing every ball (or spinning plate) to drop. There was no room for sick kids, broken-down cars, and traffic jams. There was no room for a deep breath. There was no room for community building. And most importantly, there was no room for God to move and for him to move me. While there is much to say about the epidemic of busyness, let me share what I have learned after walking away from a calendar packed beyond measure: days planned within an inch of their life leave no room for actual life.

I learned that my calendar needed to be radically rearranged in two ways: margin and honoring time with friends. *Margin*, as defined by *Merriam-Webster*, is "a spare amount allowed or given for contingencies or special situations." Margin is literally the white space on your calendar, and mine had none. When I was in the throes of sorting this out in my life, I made sure to schedule less, knowing I would need space to invest in these growing relationships. Preparing well for friendship looks like having room to be available, and that requires margin. After implementing more margin into my days, I saw the fruit of that decision almost immediately. I was no longer frantic and running everywhere. I was able to see a friend in need and had the time to sit and talk or pray as I encountered her. This was a gift!

Preparing well for friendship works when you consider it a priority. This is something I struggled with for a long time. I viewed time with friends as frivolous—sometimes even as a waste of time. Because I didn't truly value the time I spent with friends, I would easily cancel plans or not make an effort to show up. Once I got past the notion that this was a frivolous exercise, something that could be brushed aside, it became much easier for me to hold the time as valuable. Accepting the importance of this community-building work also alleviates any guilt you may have in doing something seemingly for yourself (which actually pays off big-time in the long run for you and the people around you). That was a big one for me! Navigating and nurturing a Breaking Bread Community is kingdom work that warrants time and attention.

Looping your spouse, roommate, or family into the planning and scheduling proves very helpful as well. If you want to invest time in your friendships, talk to these important people about what that might look like time-wise and get on board with the idea together. This conversation enables your support system to understand your priorities and come alongside you. The great news is that when your friendship and community needs are being met by the ones God has designed to meet them, you become a better spouse, sister, roommate. As my husband, Josh, can attest, I am a much more loving, understanding, and supportive partner on this side of my community building than I was as a lonely, longing friendly.

HOW TO MAKE PLANS

Once we have prepared our minds (and calendars!) that this community building is going to require time, we then need to decide how we are going to go about it.

We women spend a lot of time talking about getting together rather than actually getting together. Have you noticed this? "Sure, I'd love to grab a coffee" was uttered out of my mouth so often. Or "Yes, let's meet up!" Responses like this are just as superficial as the exchange "How are you?" and "I'm good." Mere pleasantries. Now, there is nothing wrong with being pleasant, of course. But pleasantries will not get you closer to your Breaking Bread Community.

This time it isn't going to be about the pleasantries. The habit of casually mentioning or agreeing to get-togethers, while well-intentioned, actually creates distance between would-be good friends when we don't follow through. When we merely talk about getting together, with no plan in place to actually gather, we are maintaining a superficial relationship. And superficial is not what we are after! Rather than saying, "Sure, let's do that sometime," you can make a plan and prepare to gather.

As we discussed in Chapter Two, when we step into Breaking Bread Community with authenticity and intention, we will become a better friend to everyone. This will manifest itself by honoring others' time and others' words, as well as our own. As we become women who engage in this type of community, we will respond with grace and honesty when offered a get-together that doesn't work and will accept the invites that do with commitment, not because we need to dig deep with everyone, but because we know that our goal is to draw near to the ones God has chosen for us.

When we follow up these invitations with intention and commitment, we are taking a step into community and friendship. We demonstrate the value of the other person, which is incredibly life-giving. When you say to someone, let's get a date settled to meet up, and then you stick with it, that person knows she is important. She knows that she matters enough for you to actually make it happen. When we get out our calendar and make a commitment to get together, it takes just a moment more, but the gesture offers a clear desire to gather and a commitment to that person. Communicating value is important when building a Breaking Bread Community.

Handling extended and accepted offers like this will also rid you of the guilt that comes when you have missed the mark with someone. Guilt is a horrible by-product of all those missed opportunities to gather with someone or of having unwittingly led her on. We say we want to get together, but then life happens and we don't follow through, and now we have this thick coating of guilt draped over the whole interaction. I've been there more times than I care to count. The "Yes, lets!" slips out of my mouth, and I know. I know it may likely never happen. Then I see her at school or at church and smile sheepishly, knowing I never did what I said I would. And the guilt wraps around me whispering lies. Lies such as *I am not good at friendship. What was I thinking? Why would I put myself into the position of ever suggesting I would meet up? I am sure there is no way to create a real friendship now.* And on and on and on. I'm left, me and my guilt, feeling more disconnected than ever.

I'm guessing you have been there, too. Guilt has no place when we are investing in God-designed communities, so we are going to prepare well and abolish guilt at the same time!

The best way I have found to avoid this cycle of missed opportunities, awkward exchanges, and impending guilt is to find a way to gather that has rhythm and reliability. Building community requires face-to-face time; there is no way around it. If we are making that time a priority, the next challenge is to ensure the get-togethers happen. This is one of the reasons the Birthday Club concept works. We know when celebrations are happening because they are tied to a specific month.

When I was just sticking my toes in the waters of community, I had a standing date with two friends. It started out as a onetime meet-up to help get a Bible study prepped. Kristen, who was leading this new study at our church, had a lot of papers to assemble, so Becky and I agreed to meet her at a coffee shop and lend a hand. As we sat there sipping our lattes, stapling, sorting, and sharing stories of our week, it felt like a blessing to be there together. The workload was minimized, and we had a few hours of child-free time to connect with one another. Becky wisely suggested we do this again, and from there, we established our standing time together. It was always the second Tuesday of the month. We knew if we had a date that we could count on, then it would be easier to hold the space on our calendar. Some months we met at a coffee shop and worked on our computers or stapled papers for a ministry; other months we would run errands together or fill out our Christmas cards. It didn't matter what we were doing, as long as we held the space to be together. We demonstrate value and create bonds by spending time together, and the only way to do that is to prepare for it.

There are many ways to incorporate rhythm and reliability in gathering. Once you find a time that works for you and your friends, replicate it! If Tuesday nights are good, then make a commitment to get together every second Tuesday. What time works for your group? Midweek brunch or perhaps dessert after the kids are tucked in? Find something that you can count on and stick with it. If the gathering has a rhythm to it and can be worked into your calendar reliably, it makes sticking to the gathering much easier. As we said, this is a commitment, and we want to make it work, so intentionality here is paramount! Spending time together with women who are called into your life in this deep way is far too important to leave to happenstance.

The Birthday Club has been, by far, my most successful, longest-standing venture into preparing well. Here is how we do it: Gather the birthdates of each friend who is committed to celebrating and share them with the group. During someone's birthday month, the honoree sends out a group text with a day, time, and place. Often, we suggest two date options and choose what works best for the majority. Everyone else's job is to do their best to attend, though we never all make every Birthday Club for the year. And that's OK! Because specifics can be helpful, here are some of our practices within the Birthday Club: We do not meet at a set time. We have met for brunch, lunch, or dinner. We split the check evenly every time—it always works out fairly and saves a lot of unnecessary figuring of the bill. We know ahead of time which months we will be gathering, so we can count on it when looking at our calendars. We hold space for these celebrations because our time together matters and we truly value celebrating one another. Some months, we may have seen each other weekly or even daily. Other months, we may not have gathered since the last Birthday Club. Either way, something very special happens when we gather in this intentional way.

If the Birthday Club concept doesn't resonate with you, that's OK! It is by no means the only way to create a Breaking Bread Community. Here are some other options that mimic the functionality of the Birthday Club:

- Book club: Choose books to read together, then gather to discuss them. The addition of reading outside of group time can make it tricky to connect, so be sure to establish flexibility in your expectations.
- Monthly cooking club: Gather everyone together for a themed night of trying new foods.
- Brunch gathering: Drop the kids at school and meet for a regular catch-up.
- Museum tour: Visit local museums and then share a pot of tea afterward.
- Garden gathering: Plot, plant, and grow your gardens together.

It doesn't matter what it is—just make a plan to gather and celebrate and break bread together. Having a specific plan that has rhythms and reliability will make extending the invitation that much easier, and that is where we are headed next!

MEET ME AT THE TABLE

Luke 22 is an amazing passage of Scripture. The humanness of the disciples, the intentionality of Jesus, and the importance of the Passover are all on display.

> Jesus sent Peter and John, saying, "Go and make preparations for us to eat the Passover."
>
> "Where do you want us to prepare for it?" they asked.
>
> He replied, "As you enter the city, a man carrying a jar of water will meet you. Follow him to the house that he enters, and say to the owner of the house, 'The Teacher asks: Where is the guest room, where I may eat the Passover with my disciples?' He will show you a large room upstairs, all furnished. Make preparations there."
>
> They left and found things just as Jesus had told them. So they prepared the Passover. (Luke 22:8–13)

We are going to break down this passage into three types of preparation, but here is what I see when I read through it. Jesus gives directions to Peter and John, and their immediate response is, "How do you expect us to do that?" To which Jesus replies, "Don't worry! I've set you up for success. I've held space for you, and you just need to go and be intentional." And then, it all works out exactly as Jesus tells them. Amen.

We can see how important preparing well was to Jesus and the disciples. The word for prepare in Greek, *hetoimazō*, is used four times in this short passage. *Hetoimazō* means to prepare, provide, and make ready. Preparations mattered for the Last Supper.

Passover, in particular, is a rather intricate meal that does require specific preparation. While some contest that the Lord's Supper may not have been a traditional Passover based on timing, it likely included the Passover dishes of the time—many still used in seders to do this day. Charoset (a delicious fruit and nut dish), bitter herbs dipped in salt water, wine, and unleavened bread all would have been present. Surely the disciples would have needed to prepare for the supper. However, as we examine this passage in detail, we see several layers of preparation, all being used to knit this community of friends together. We see preparation in the form of setting up the disciples for success. We see preparation in the form of holding space. We also see preparation in the form of taking care and being intentional.

This is the answer to our question, "How can I possibly do this?" Set yourself and your friends up for success, hold space, and be intentional.

Setting Up for Success

In Luke 22:10, Jesus says, "As you enter the city, a man carrying a jar of water will meet you. Follow him to the house that he enters." There are a few things going on here that are particularly interesting. I love the notion of this prearranged meeting.

It reminds me of the scene from the movie *You've Got Mail*, where Kathleen Kelly has a book and a rose on the corner of her table at the café so her suitor can recognize her. Jesus tells his disciples to look for the man carrying a jug of water because that task would have stood out in the environment. Men at that time were not charged with the filling of jugs of water. Even further, some commentators have speculated that the jug itself was an anomaly, as many had sheepskin bags for water transport.

The point is this: Jesus prepared this meet-up in such a way that the disciples would know, without a shadow of doubt, whom to ask. Jerusalem was incredibly crowded at this time, and to find one person might have been a challenging task. By using an unlikely person, something we see Jesus do often, it was as if he placed a beacon of light above the man they were to seek out. They were then set up for success all due to Jesus's preparation.

How often do we miss the chance to help our friends gather successfully? One way we can prepare well for our friends to gather is by setting them up for success. It seems counterintuitive, I know, but if we take just a bit of time to think through what might make our plans easier for our friends, we will all actually benefit. Our community bonds will grow even deeper during our gatherings. Now, of course, this is going to look quite different for us than it did for Jesus and the disciples. What beacons can we shine to make the act of gathering easier? This can look like a friendly reminder text before meeting, setting up group childcare so that everyone can attend, remembering dietary restrictions when choosing a restaurant, or choosing a day and time that works well with their family schedule.

A small bit of preparation on our part helps convey value to our friends. A text saying, "Hey, the driveway to the restaurant isn't lit well, but you will see it after the third stoplight," may seem simple, and it is. But what it offers is profound. Letting your community know that you care for them and want them to gather with you as successfully and stress-free as possible creates trust, reliance, and connectedness. What beacon (what man with the jug of water) can you point out that will ensure your friends don't get lost on the way to gathering, both literally and figuratively?

Sadly, I have been the one, more than once, to disregard the value of preparing well in this way. I've made plans to meet dear friends, driven hours, and asked them to do the same, only to discover that the meeting place I had chosen was closed or had switched hours or had canceled an exhibit. Here is how it played out: every time we scrambled to rework an outing, I apologized like crazy and felt awful, with my friend making sure I didn't feel bad and sweetly overcompensating. Of course, this was not a deal-breaker in the way of friendship, and there have been many other times when we happened upon a similar circumstance and it felt like a great adventure. What makes this exact scenario hard is that it reflects my lack of care. I asked someone to drive two hours and never bothered to ensure the museum was open. I asked someone to drive with her kids and never considered where we might eat.

Had I taken a moment to prepare well, to set us up for success, the value and love I have for my friends would have been communicated clearly. How easy is it to love a friend by calling to ensure the hours are as listed on the website? How easy is it to set a mama friend up for a coffee date by choosing a location with a play area for her little ones? Preparing well by setting each other up for success looks a lot like loving our friends well, and that builds Breaking Bread Communities.

Holding Space

In Luke 22:12, Jesus says, "He will show you a large room upstairs, all furnished. Make preparations there." Ah, the Upper Room. It sounds like a magical place, doesn't it? We know it certainly became the center point, not just of this evening but of the next weeks as the disciples continued to use this space for gathering. In this one verse, we see the value of preparing well by holding space.

To understand how this verse is a reflection of preparing well, it is important to realize what Jerusalem looked like on the day Jesus sent them to go and find a furnished room. It was Passover, a pilgrimage festival, which meant Jerusalem was filled to the brim as more and more people came to celebrate. Estimates for the total number of people in Jerusalem at that time, including those who had come to town for Passover, are as high as 2.7 million people! This is why Peter and John replied, "Where do you want us to prepare for it?" They were saying that Jesus was asking the impossible—there was no room in the city. If you wanted to celebrate Passover in Jerusalem, you likely had a plan a year in advance for exactly where you would be celebrating. This would *not* be the time to show up and sort it out! The disciples believed that this was what Jesus was asking them to do, to find space where there was none. But not Jesus. He had a place set aside, ready and prepared for his friends to gather.

Now here is where things get interesting for us. I am going to argue that our calendars are the Jerusalem of our time. Stuffed and overrun. And our job as those seeking community is to hold space. We must hold space for our Breaking Bread Communities and prepare to welcome others well. I know we have already covered the busyness epidemic in this chapter, but boy does it take on new meaning when we see how Christ held space. We have prayed for friends to be made known to us, and now we must have time set aside to engage with them. Let's prepare our calendars well by holding space. This is where the rhythms and reliability prove to be helpful. Times and days we can count on make it easier for us to hold space.

Being Intentional

Now we come to the actual Passover preparations and how we must prepare well by taking care, by being intentional. "They left and found things just as Jesus had told them. So they prepared the Passover" (Luke 22:13).

Preparing for Passover was no small thing. The menu was set, full of specific items to be purchased: bitter herbs, unleavened bread, and eggs. And charoset (my favorite), a fruit and nut paste, was to be made, among many other items. Our family has celebrated a Passover dinner on Maundy Thursday for a few years now, and it is the best holiday meal, according to our children. The rich symbolism is incredibly moving, the unusual foods are exciting, and the parsley dipped in salt water is the kids' favorite "dish." What stands out about the meal is that every single thing on the plate has purpose. The preparations are intense and specific. They require extra care, as does the laying out of the items on the table and the time spent as we work our way through the meal. Unabashed intentionality.

That is what is required of us as we set forth on this venture to dive deep into a Breaking Bread Community. We need to be unabashedly intentional. For example, I often write "connect with a friend" on my weekly goals. Setting the goal on paper, for me, holds me accountable and creates intentionality. I could feel badly about my need to be so specific in my goal setting, as if it is proof of my ineptitude at friendship, *or* I can claim it as proof that I am serious about my friendships. It is OK that friendship building requires our best effort. Intentionality takes effort, and there is no way around that. If we want deeper friendships, it will require more of us to make it happen. We are going after the good stuff and that, by nature, will demand time and intentionality. But it is so worth it!

And let's not forget the best promise we also find in our verses. They left and found things just as Jesus had told them. *That* is what we are after! The shift in my friendships occurred once I got comfortable with the fact that this was going to take intentionality.

Once I began preparing well, the friendships I found were just as Jesus told me. Amen, indeed.

Let it be so for you as well. Be unabashedly intentional and prepare well.

BREAK BREAD TOGETHER

After studying God's Word, we will spend time reflecting, praying, and preparing to take action. Let's have our friendships transformed by our time in the Word!

1. Examine the stumbling blocks you find when making concrete plans with friends. Is it a lack of an accurate calendar? Not enough time? Saying it when we don't mean it?

2. What changes can you make to ensure you are holding time for focusing on friendship?

3. What type of gathering would you like to enjoy with your community?

4. Make a plan to gather and continue gathering with friends. Remember to make it based on rhythms and reliability.

5. What specifically will you do to prepare well for your next
   gathering?

Lord,

We see the importance of preparing well. We see the way
Jesus and the disciples prepared to gather together. Father,
help us to clear the way in our own lives. Help us to make
room to prepare. As we begin to imagine these gatherings
and celebrations, Lord, will you place a specific vision on
our hearts? How do you want us to gather and celebrate?
Help us be women who prepare well for others to come
into our homes, into our lives, into our hearts. Amen.

CHAPTER FIVE

SERVE AND RECEIVE WELL

I have found there is no greater way to bind a community together than service. Cultivating a culture of service leads to deeper community. This culture of service manifests itself by being a humble servant and also by welcoming others' service in your life. I personally thrive on the former and am continually challenged by the latter.

For my birthday, my sister gifted me with an amazing pair of shoes. They were red suede d'orsay flats with a tassel from a favorite store. They are a luxury I never would have bought myself. Fun and classic, they "make" any outfit I wear them with. The very next day I wore my brand-new shoes to my moms' group at church. They were, perhaps, a bit splashy for the occasion, but I was eager to brighten up my outfit and enjoy my new kicks. That morning before I left for the meeting, I took several pics of my new shoes because I was just so excited to have them.

I, of course, received lots of compliments on the red shoes. As we were catching each other up on the comings and goings of our families, my friend Kathy mentioned she had a work party to attend that evening. We asked what the party was like and what she was wearing, and as she filled us in on her evening plans, she mentioned that she had yet to find the right shoes to wear with her dress. She described what she was looking for, and we realized my new shoes fit the bill perfectly. She jokingly said they would be perfect, and without hesitation, I said, "Take them." We are the same shoe size, so I knew she could actually use them. There was no hesitation on my part because it was my delight to share the shoes and serve my friend. Even though they were brand-new and my dream shoes, I truly wanted her to use them.

So, at the end of the meeting, Kathy followed me out to my car, and I handed her the shoes off my feet and drove home barefoot. On the way back to my house, I took a pic of my bare feet. Let me tell you, the pictures of my beloved shoes pale in comparison to that picture of my bare feet. Not because I was glorifying my "sacrifice," but because I delight in knowing that I have friendships that allow me to give the shoes off my feet.

Service among friends can be as simple and silly as that. I have what you need, and it is my delight to serve you. And it truly is a delight to serve your friends. Serving is a way of growing connection and trust within a Breaking Bread Community. To be able to serve one another, we must first notice what other people need. It is in the noticing that we grow trust between friends. It is in the noticing that we forge deeper, stronger connections by letting our friends know, "I see you and you matter to me."

"Big" moments of service—when there is a major life event, like a new baby or a death in the family, and meals are needed or when there are trials requiring prayer and assistance—are all wonderful, impactful things. But if we let our sense of service stop there we miss out. We have, somehow, come to believe that service is something to be scheduled, planned, and prioritized only when there are major life events. But a true culture of service is noticing and stepping in over and over again; it is lots of small moments that, together, create something big.

Imagine the difference between flowers given on Valentine's Day and flowers given on a "normal" week when you are in need of a pick-me-up. The pick-me-up flowers mean much more because they required noticing! We can do that for our friends. It is such a joy to meet with a friend you know has had a particularly busy week and have something prepared for them to eat for dinner. I've even invited a friend over for a playdate and then showed her to our guest room so that she could take a nap because I knew her sleep at the time was minimal. If I hadn't been noticing what was going on in her life, I might have missed that easy yet impactful way to serve her.

The other side of living in a culture of service with your friends is that you must be a willing recipient of service. Yes, I said *must*. This is infinitely harder for me, personally, so we will work through this one together because I am sure I am not alone here. It can be hard to receive service well, even from beloved friends. I am self-reliant to a fault. I am (or at least I can be) hard and abrasive, demanding, exacting, and overwhelmingly capable of handling a lot. But just because I *can* do it all does not mean I was *designed* to do it all on my own. In fact, extreme self-reliance damages friendships and community. It is hurtful to hear that a friend was struggling when I could have helped. I have also been the friend who has caused distance by not bringing my friends into my struggles and asking for help. They would have loved to be included and serve me, but I robbed them of the opportunity. That hurts! Think about that. If you struggle with asking for help or receiving help and doing it well, you are hurting your relationships. Self-reliance, in this regard, is another way of building a wall, which makes it difficult for others to get inside and know us deeply. Ouch.

I have felt like I was drowning and still didn't know how to say, "Hey, I could use some help over here!" When asked, the answer was always "I'm fine. We're good." And yes, maybe I was fine. But was I thriving? No. Was I the best I could be in that given situation? Also no. Would my life have been improved by welcoming some help into my world? Yes. So why is receiving service well so hard? I believe it comes down to fear or shame. Most wall building comes from one of the two, if not both. Let's tear down some walls.

Resisting others' service is often based on the fear that things won't be done the way we want or at least the way we planned. We have all heard the saying, "If you want something done right, do it yourself." (Can I get an *amen* from all the Type As?) It can be a battle cry or a shout of solidarity among all of us who grasp control of everything in our white-knuckled fists. Of course, we need to do it all—everyone else will mess it up. But this is absolutely counter to Jesus's desire for us and for our relationships. This popular phrase is actually a mistranslation of a quote by playwright Charles-Guillaume Étienne. The literal translation is, "One is never served so well as by oneself." Well, that doesn't sound so cute. I know I am not the one who will serve me the best. I also know I don't want to live a life so focused on myself and what I, alone, can do for me. Stripped down to its actual meaning, we see the self-focused, misguided nature of this thinking.

In our effort to tear down walls and welcome service into our lives, let's start by acknowledging that the value in the help far outweighs our fear of having things done in a way we wouldn't plan. Things will not be done the way we prefer or would have planned ourselves, but the goodness found in allowing others to step fully into our lives wins every time. The alternative is to believe a self-focused way is the best way, and I don't want that for you or for me.

Shame is another huge component in resisting service from others. For whatever reason, many of us believe the lie that we are supposed to do everything and do it all well. When we receive help or, even more, raise our hand and ask for help, there is a sense that we have somehow missed the mark. Embarrassment and, yes, shame creep in and whisper to us that we ought to be able to handle things on our own. That we have failed. But here is the truth: we were not designed to go it alone. You are a created being designed by a loving Father who made you for community—made you to need and serve other people. When we accept service in our lives, it is an admission that we cannot do everything alone. This reality can be used to shame us if we believe the lie, or it can be used to point us to Christ if we believe in our design.

What if instead of sheepishly, shamefully acknowledging that we can't do everything ourselves, we instead used the truth as an affirmation of community? What if we used it as a way to draw us nearer to our friends rather than building walls to keep them at bay? That is where true community is found.

My friend Heather is an amazing example to me of living in service-centered community. We (half) joke that her ultimate dream is to live in a commune with her friends and their families. A sweet culture of service and community overflows out of her and into a dreamlike vision of life together. She reminds me how good it is to be involved in one another's lives. She serves others so well and has humbly, graciously allowed me and others to serve her in return. The trust and connections her willingness to serve and be served have developed are such a beautiful thing.

When I look at my closest friends, my community, I am reminded that when God chose them for me, he knew their giftings and therefore knew how their giftings would specifically bless me. Think about that for a moment. If God chose our community, then the people in our community were designed to specifically bless us and us them. Their giftings will bless our lives in specific ways that we may not be able to imagine when we first invite them into community. To think that we could be robbing ourselves of this opportunity is sobering.

Heather has shown up for me and my family in crazy specific ways throughout our friendship. I would never have predicted that a friend who is a crisis counselor would be needed in my life for that exact skill, but she has. My life and those around me are better because she was there and because I said *yes* when she asked if she could help. That is an amazing benefit of God-designed friendships.

MEET ME AT THE TABLE

When we think of service and modeling Jesus in our friendships and community, there may be no greater example than that of the foot washing that takes place at the Last Supper. As we study this familiar scene, we are reminded why we serve, how we serve, and how to receive service, as well as the call to step into service within our communities.

> Jesus, knowing that the Father had given all things into his hands, and that he had come from God and was going back to God, rose from supper. He laid aside his outer garments, and taking a towel, tied it around his waist. Then he poured water into a basin and began to wash the disciples' feet and to wipe them with the towel that was wrapped around him. (John 13:3–5 ESV)

The act of washing feet was about as lowly as it could get. It was a job reserved for the lowest servants in the household; oftentimes even Jewish servants were not asked to do the job, as it was considered beneath them.

So here was Jesus, about to step into the same position, and why was he doing this? The motivation for Jesus's service can be found in the beginning of our text. Because he knew. Jesus knew what he had, knew who he was, and knew where he was going. Equipped with that knowledge, he served. When we too know what we have and that everything has been given to us by God; when we know who we are, that we are daughters of the King; and when we know where we are going, that heaven awaits us; then we will be compelled to serve. True service flows from the abundance and security of knowing. The verse tells us that Jesus knew the Father and that the Father had given him all power. It is that omnipotent, almighty position that motivates Christ to get down on his hands and knees and serve. There is nothing lowly about it. Service, as Jesus shows us, demonstrates the authority and majesty and power of God in our own lives.

As you step out into a role of service with your friends, remember that you too have the honor of representing God's power and your closeness to him by allowing others to benefit from your service. Your service is a reflection of God and the goodness and assurance that comes from being a daughter of the King. So what does service look like? Again, we look to Jesus as he washed the disciples' feet. As you read slowly through the next sections, you will notice a lot of verbs, action words. That is what service ultimately has to be: action. Let's look at the specific things Christ did and how we can apply them to serving our community today.

He Rose from Supper

I can only imagine how startled and curious the disciples were when the leader of the meal suddenly rose up from supper. This was an interruption. And like all interruptions, it was unexpected. But it was an interruption that Jesus initiated and welcomed. How many times do we see service to a friend as an interruption in how we thought our day would go? What if we welcomed the interruption as an opportunity to stop and serve? Jesus rose from supper with joy and purpose, ready to serve.

Laid Aside His Outer Garments

We could spend a lot of time discussing garments here and the significance of each layer. The key is that the verse says "outer garments." This layer of dress was perhaps the most valuable. It was a shawl or cloak that was most valuable as a cover for travelers—often their only means of comfort as they slept. The outer garments were held aside in Jewish law as being off-limits, meaning they could not legally be taken away as punishment since they were so necessary.

And what did Jesus do? He laid it aside. Willing, eager even, to give up what was considered the most valuable garment so that he could serve his community best. What do we need to lay aside to better step into a posture of service? Could it be our calendars or schedule? Our car or home? Jesus first laid aside what the world held as valuable to make room for better service.

Tied a Towel around His Waist

After rising up and then laying down his garments, Jesus tied a towel around his waist. In other words, he prepared for the job ahead. We just spent a great deal of time on the value of preparing well, so I won't belabor the point here, but in regard to service specifically, what do you need to do to prepare for the job?

If you are going to serve your friend by working in her garden, did you bring gardening gloves? If you are going to serve your friend by simply being available to listen, is your phone turned off? Service is an act, and it helps to suit up for the job to do it well. Jesus wrapped his waist with a towel, and in that small act, his friends could see he was serious about serving because he was ready and prepared.

Began to Wash

And now the actual service begins. Remember these men were dirty and lying low on the ground. This was an intimate act that Jesus stepped right into, fully. The teacher bowing low to clean the day's dirt off the disciples' feet. He did not shy away from it but instead began to wash and then dry each foot.

In the same way, when there is service that we can offer, we are called to get to it. When I have a sink full of dishes (almost always) and a friend jumps into the pile and starts washing, I am so blessed. There is something beautiful about acts of service that are truly filled with action. So get in there and get washing.

HOW WE RECEIVE SERVICE

The Last Supper provides us with not only a beautiful example of stepping into service but also an example of receiving service.

> He came to Simon Peter, who said to him, "Lord, do you wash my feet?" Jesus answered him, "What I am doing you do not understand now, but afterward you will understand." Peter said to him, "You shall never wash my feet." Jesus answered him, "If I do not wash

you, you have no share with me." Simon Peter said to
him, "Lord, not my feet only but also my hands and my
head!" (John 13:6–9 ESV)

In this passage, we see Peter model how *not* to receive service. Oh, Peter. I adore his humanness and relate to him so very often. As Jesus bent down in this act of service, Peter was appalled and even declared that he would never have Jesus wash his feet. There is a mix of shame and pride that results in a refusal of service. It is as if Peter was saying, "I can't accept anything from you." Jesus was willingly offering, and poor Peter didn't know how to accept.

Renowned theologian and archbishop William Temple has said, "Man's humility does not begin with the giving of service; it begins with the readiness to receive it." I find it amazing to consider the degree of humility required to receive such an act of service from Christ. To know, wholeheartedly, you are not worthy and still to receive the act with grace is to receive the gift of Christ himself.

This plays out in our friendships and communities in a similar way. We disqualify our friends by assuming they are too busy or have more important things to do. In so doing, we are essentially saying, "I can't accept anything from you," just like Peter. When we disqualify them, we are stripping them of the opportunity to serve, to bless and to serve like Jesus. Perhaps we are embarrassed or feel shame because, truth be told, we do need the help. Perhaps we are prideful because we can't admit, even to ourselves, that we would benefit from the service.

What if instead of refusing service, we acknowledge that our friends *are* busy and *do* have important things to do, and that we get to be one of those important things—one of the things they make time for? What if we ditched the pride that says I can do it all alone and instead welcome the service of those designed to serve us? Let's be humbler than we ever imagined possible and allow the gift of service to wash over our friendships with grace.

Our friend Peter has another lesson to teach us about how not to receive service. Once he understands the gift of service being offered, his response makes me chuckle. Once Peter understands that allowing Jesus to serve him allows him to have deeper community, Peter responds, "Don't stop with my feet!" With an almost gluttonous response, he begs Jesus to keep going for more and more. Let's take this as our reminder not to be like Peter in this way, either. When a friend offers service, let's receive it well, but let's not ask for more and more.

Sometimes when we find a willing servant, it is too easy to see *all* the ways that person could help us. Restraint and trust are required. Just as Jesus knew what the disciples needed, so too will our God-inspired friends know how to serve us well.

> If I then, your Lord and Teacher, have washed your feet, you also ought to wash one another's feet. For I have given you an example, that you also should do just as I have done to you. (John 13:14–15 ESV)

And now that we have seen service in action within a Breaking Bread Community, we have the charge to go and do this for each other. Jesus could not be more direct here. If I am doing this, then so should you. We are called to serve one another with humility, considering nothing beneath us because we know what we have, who we are, and where we are going. Blessings abound when we live in service, together.

BREAK BREAD TOGETHER

After studying God's Word, we will spend time reflecting, praying, and preparing to take action. Let's have our friendships transformed by our time in the Word!

1. Brainstorm a list of ways you can serve your friends right now. What needs have you noticed?

2. If you have received service poorly in the past, reach out and apologize for it.

3. Post a verse from the Scripture that resonates with you as a reminder to continually step into service.

4. Ask for help with something. It's hard, but you can do it and will be blessed for it!

Father,

Help us serve others well. Lord, let us be need-noticers. Give us your eyes as we see our friends so that we can step in to serve in meaningful ways as needs become apparent. And, Father, we humbly ask forgiveness for any prideful moments that have prevented us from receiving service. Lord, we pray that you break the chains of shame and fear so that we can let others in and gladly receive service from our community. We trust that you have called these specific people into our lives and wait with expectancy for the blessings their presence will be to us and the honor it will be to bless them. Amen, indeed.

CHAPTER SIX

THE GREATEST

Throughout grade school, I was the student who hated group projects. *Hated*. The energy necessary to navigate the group dynamics was always so taxing to me. On top of that, I was one of the kids who did the bulk of the work, and when it came time to present, it made me crazy to see the others in the group smiling and soaking up all the accolades that, truth be told, I thought I alone deserved. Surely, I was the hardest working and most productive, and therefore, shouldn't I have been the one to receive the praise?

The reality is that what I was really after was the credit and the glory of being the best. I wanted to affirm what I was good at and make sure it was known by those around me. As we seek our own glory, we start to keep tabs on those around us. In our humanness, we naturally seek out a way to sort ourselves compared to others. She is taller, she is smarter, she is the prettiest, she is more popular. We categorize ourselves even still, just as we did in grade school, so that we know where we rank.

This same type of ranking happens within friendship communities, and it is something to be on the lookout for. We may be quietly angling for the best-behaved kids or the cleanest homes or the most devout practices. While this type of comparison is possible, I have found it to be unlikely within Breaking Bread Communities. What more often rears its head is an angling for proximity. Within a group of even a handful of friends, certain people will break off to form a closer bond based on all sorts of things: geography, common interests, and compatible schedules, to name a few. This is to be expected and isn't unhealthy until a sense of competition or jealousy works its way into the dynamics.

My friend Kathy and I have stumbled upon a fun tradition where we get our families together for leftovers the day after Thanksgiving. It is a great way to use up all the extra food I cooked and is a no-pressure way to allow the holiday to linger a moment later. We look forward to this time together, and I even find myself making certain dishes for the main holiday, knowing they will be shared with our friends the next day. Now, I of course could include other friends in this evening, but I choose not to because it has become "our thing." I can see how keeping things tight with Kathy appears to be showing preference and also how upset feelings might arise as a result. I am sure the leftover night seems like a fun thing to be invited to, and others may be wondering why they aren't included.

I've been left out of outings as well, and from there you can see how damaging feeling left out can be, even among a group of friends. As pairings break off within a community to form even closer bonds or to have specific adventures, it can be tricky to navigate. Keeping tabs on who is closest with whom in your community can prove to be more exhausting than navigating the group project dynamics of grade school. I have experienced the sting of thinking how much I would have loved to be included on that coffee date or trip to the museum, and that sting can quickly lead to negative thoughts about your worth within the community or jealous thoughts that ultimately become a roadblock to deeper friendship. It is easy to begin to question your place among the friends you have when you allow jealousy to take root.

Why is it that when I am on the side of the one making plans, I can easily brush off that feeling of hurt or jealousy, but when I am on the side of the one being left out, I allow those emotions to grab hold? I believe the answer is that this is a very human problem!

MEET ME AT THE TABLE

Let's watch the disciples grapple with the same dynamics and learn from Jesus how to navigate this question of who is the greatest.

> A dispute also arose among them as to which of them was considered to be greatest. Jesus said to them, "The kings of the Gentiles lord it over them; and those who exercise authority over them call themselves Benefactors. But you are not to be like that. Instead, the greatest among you should be like the youngest, and the one who rules like the one who serves. (Luke 22:24–26)

Even after living with and walking with and learning from Jesus directly and personally for years, jealousy and competition came bubbling up out of the disciples. They were altogether human. In fact, this was not the first time this issue had come up with them. We also see this discussion of who is the greatest in Matthew 18:1, Mark 9:33–34, and Luke 9:46. There was also a moment where James and John, through their mother, petitioned Jesus for places of importance, namely sitting on his right and his left

(Matt. 20:20–26), and that petition led to . . . more arguing about who was the greatest.

The comforting thing to see and hear is that squabbles and unrest of this nature, or even hurt feelings, are entirely predictable and are not indicators of an inherently flawed community. In other words, we are all going to be OK. If the disciples struggled with this, how much more likely are we to struggle? Thankfully, on this last night of his earthly ministry, Jesus very patiently redirected the disciples' thinking, and in so doing he offered guidance for us today. The problem wasn't so much the squabbling of the disciples. They were, as your Breaking Bread Community will be also, a group of wildly diverse people, and one of the challenges of gathering a group of different people together is to get them all on the same page. So as disputes and different points of view crop up, handle them well, but don't take them as a sign of trouble. The trouble begins when we start keeping score.

When it comes to the scorekeeping, Jesus had something specific to say. The first thing Jesus pointed out was who *else* partakes in scorekeeping, ranking, and keeping tabs on people. In Luke 22:25, Jesus showed us that this is the behavior of Gentile monarchy, of the power-hungry eager to lord their power over those they deem subservient. And then he minces no words: "You are not to be like that." Jesus reminds us that our natural inclination toward power and position, even among beloved friends, causes us to live by worldly standards. The friendships we are called to build will reflect God's kingdom, and that can be done by resisting the urge to vie for position and to keep score. And then Jesus offered a better way: "For who is the greater, one who reclines at table or one who serves? Is it not the one who reclines at table? But I am among you as the one who serves" (Luke 22:27 ESV).

Jesus so patiently showed the disciples another way to handle intergroup dynamics, and in so doing, he flipped the entire concept of greatness on its head. As the disciples were bickering over who among them was the best, Jesus asked them to look around. Here he was, serving them boldly, and yet he was the one deserving of all adoration. Jesus showed them how service changes everything. There is no angling for superiority when you are on your hands and knees as a servant. The entire concept of service as an equalizer is entirely countercultural. This is where a culture of service, as we talked about in the previous chapter, becomes so important to the health of your community. Service negates scorekeeping and causes us to seek what is best for our friends.

Where we could feel left out, instead we see that these smaller groupings of friends are filling a specific need for each other. Kathy and I have a lot in common within our larger family dynamics, as do our husbands, and so we understand demands placed on us in a way that others may not. When they approach the group through the lens of service, our other friends can see how those similarities serve her and me specifically and so, rather than holding on to jealousy, they celebrate them. And I too do the same thing when I see friends who have a closer relationship than I do with them. I am thankful for how that friendship blesses them specifically in ways I may not be equipped to.

This attitude leads to unity, and that is the goal for any group of believers, in particular those living in close community. At the very end of that evening, Jesus prayed to God, and as he prayed specifically for the disciples, he prayed for unity among them (John 17:11). He asked for protection over the group so that they might be one. As we continue to focus on service over scorekeeping, unity will flourish within our own communities as well.

BREAK BREAD TOGETHER

After studying God's Word, we will spend time reflecting, praying, and preparing to take action. Let's have our lives transformed by our time in the Word!

1. Have you ever experienced jealousy within a group of friends?

2. How can you reframe it as an acceptable reality that there will naturally be inner dynamics within any group of friends?

3. How does service negate the competition aspect that can occur within community?

4. How does Jesus act as the great equalizer?

Father,

*Thank you for these wonderful flawed humans that were
called into community with Jesus. Through their flaws
we can see ourselves, and for that we are thankful. Help
us to assume a posture of servitude within our own
communities. Lord, let us focus there rather than on our
position within the group. Root out any jealousy within us.
In your kingdom there are seats at the table for all of us.
As we wait for that day, help us to live out the culture of
service within our own communities so that we may serve
our friends and reflect you. Amen, indeed.*

CHAPTER SEVEN

GET
MESSY

I don't mean to brag or anything, but my life is very messy. It is full of messes. These messes have been a big roadblock in my fully stepping into community. I define "messes" as the challenges, complications, trials, and parts of our lives that are not neat or tidy. And as I said, I have a very messy life. I am willing to bet that I am not alone in this. In fact, I know I am not alone. We all have messy lives. Maybe your mess looks different than mine, but nonetheless the mess is there.

For a long time, I allowed the messes of my life to prevent me from engaging with friendships. That was a big reason I was left with surface-level friends and no true community. When I began investing in community, I realized that I had been building walls around me to hide my mess. Yes, more walls. We aren't done tearing walls down quite yet. Since I was married in 2005, I have yet to experience a twelve-month span without a major family crisis. I spent a long time being the girl with the dead mother, the complicated family, the ill sister or nephew or brother or dad, the one who always has some crisis going on. Crises do seem to surround us constantly. Even during the span of writing this book, my dad experienced a sudden decline and passed. I am truly not exaggerating when I tell you my life is messy. I pray yours isn't more so than mine, but I know for sure there are those that are messier still.

Here is a hard truth: a complicated life is intimidating to many people. I say that with no judgment; it is simply a reality. As the history of my family unfolds in normal conversation, I have learned how to gauge people's discomfort. I am always aware of their response and then discern how much I share. Can they handle what I am saying? Have they started to cry? Maybe they are holding their hand up to their mouth or have even taken an actual step backward. I know the signs, and I can perceive when they have reached capacity. Dealing with someone's overwhelmed response to your own life is, well, overwhelming. So I have learned to hold back, and in so doing I have taught myself another lie: I am too messy for people.

Have you been the one who *always* has a prayer request? Yep, that's me. What a strange thing to have to manage. I have, in the past, actually not asked for prayer because I didn't want to be the one always asking. Imagine that. Needing prayer and feeling so aware of your neediness that you don't ask for fear of . . . what, exactly? Fear of being seen as too messy to handle. In those moments when I have shared, I have sighed with disbelief as I send out another prayer request asking for more miracles, sharing more tragedies, praying that my friends don't grow weary of me. When I am unwilling to ask for prayer, I am for sure believing the lie that my friends can't handle my mess.

I once sat in a moms' group where a friend admitted that she hadn't changed her sheets in several months. It was one of the bravest things I have ever heard someone admit. It was truth. And it was messy. And she shared anyway. In that moment, we all felt so honored to be let into her mess. There was no judgment or condemnation or even pity. There was understanding and solidarity.

Watching that happen allowed me to see how much of my mess I was hiding, not just the big crisis messes but all of the mess of living life. It also helped me examine the root of my isolation. It occurred to me that I had predetermined what was too much for my friends. Now, remember, we are talking about a Breaking Bread Community—a God-designed group of people who were prayed for and invited into my life and me into theirs. Even still, I was holding back. As one crisis after another cropped up, I realized that I would pick up the phone, or type out a message updating a friend on something, and then delete the whole thing, convinced the friend, the one God chose for me, couldn't handle the messy reality of my life. I am so sad just remembering that. Wanting community, having community, and not feeling free enough to say, "Hey, this is what's going on with me right now." The only way I have been able to step fully into community is by allowing others to see the full mess of my life, on the messiest days and the not-so-messy days alike.

The other pesky thing that gets in the way for me is shame. When our lives are chaotic, crisis-filled, or simply not going well, it is easy to carry shame or embarrassment about it. Shame comes from believing that our lives are "supposed to be" one way and that they are not meeting the mark. I feel embarrassed because when everyone else can say yes to a playdate or a night out, I have to once again say no because my family's needs are constant. I feel embarrassed because I have to work around a more complicated schedule or am tethered to my house as a caretaker for my dad. I feel embarrassed because I believe I am letting others down when my life is simply missing the mark of easy and normal. Not only that, but the embarrassment is embarrassing in itself, and thus a vicious cycle is built brick by brick as I build my wall and then retreat behind it. The shame, embarrassment, fear, and protection that we feel about our mess isolate us as we worry about others' reactions to the untidy parts of our lives.

This shame can creep in when we are talking about little daily messes, too. Literal messes. For example, a sink full of dirty dishes, dust bunnies the size of Texas, a kitchen counter covered in mounds of papers. All of which are continual messes I battle in my own home. These may seem insignificant, but I am going to address them because, well, they can be a literal reason we aren't letting people in the door. I grew up with an amazing mom who taught me all sorts of incredible lessons about family, faith, relationships, service, and hospitality, but just about zero lessons on keeping a home. I am not naturally gifted at it, and neither was she. It is work that I am more often than not quite behind on. I used to have dreams of friends just popping by to say hello like they did in the 1950s sitcoms. The dream didn't last long, though, because I then realized my house would need to be visitor-ready *all the time*. Yikes.

There have been times when a friend sent a text because she was close by and wanted to drop something off or say a quick hello, and I have said, "No, thanks." Requests like that were pain-inducing. *Please don't come over here; we are too messy. Thank you very much.* I am sad just remembering those moments. I missed out on precious face-to-face time because of dust bunnies. What I have found is that when I realized an untidy house was *never* a good reason to skip a visit with a friend, I actually began to live out my dream of friendly visitors. My amazing friend Amy has even said she finds comfort in being at our home partly because it's never perfect. Hallelujah! The mess no longer stops me from saying yes.

Here is the good news that I have learned: if you are investing in your God-chosen people, they will not be freaked out by your mess! It will not be too much for them—you do not need to be embarrassed or carry shame with them. They were designed to be in this community with you, designed to handle your mess with grace and love and mercy. Doesn't it sound too good to be true? Let me assure you it is truer than you could ever realize and waiting for you to fully step into. Your house does not need to be visitor-ready; it needs to be friend-ready.

Now let's look at the other side of the coin. Raise your hand if you have ever thought, "I could be friends with her, except . . ." I'm guilty, too. Maybe you tolerate your own messy life quite well, but it is other people's messes that give you pause. Well, what is good for the goose is good for the gander. In other words, "our" people's messes cannot dissuade us from stepping into deep friendship. Life is messy—yours, mine, all of ours—and so we must welcome each other's messes into our life. Will we be affected by their mess? Yes. Will our life be challenged by their mess? Possibly. Is this all part of God's design? Absolutely. Allowing someone to be herself around you means allowing her mess to impact you. God's design of a Breaking Bread Community is for us to be impacted by one another!

MEET ME AT THE TABLE

When we consider our attitude toward our own messes and the messes of our friends, John 16:33 is a great place to start.

> I have told you these things, so that in me you may have peace. In this world you will have trouble. But take heart! I have overcome the world.

When Jesus spoke these words at the Last Supper, not only were we promised trouble, or messes, but we were also promised peace. Peace! Peace to share and allow others to see our mess. We don't need to be embarrassed or hold back because of our trials. Who can be embarrassed about something we are told to expect? Jesus overcame the world, and therefore we can have a new perspective on any mess or trouble we may face. We face it with peace in our hearts. Peace casts out shame and embarrassment and allows us to tear down walls and invite others in. When we remember that trouble is expected—in fact, it's guaranteed by Jesus—we see that there is no place for shame when life gets particularly messy.

The enemy wants us silent and shameful behind our own walls. It is there that we struggle to experience the peace promised to us by Jesus in this verse. It is there that we are cut off from life-giving community. It is there that we find loneliness. We must resist the urge to hold back or hide our mess. Remembering the words of Jesus, we can shake off the shame and instead be brave and bold. Our friends will be OK. They were made for this. They want to know how we are doing, truly doing, mess and all. They will welcome us and our mess. In fact, our community is a gift that brings us peace as they point us to Christ.

When we need direction for how to respond to someone else's mess, we again turn to Jesus at the Last Supper as our example:

> Simon, Simon, behold, Satan demanded to have
> you, that he might sift you like wheat, but I have
> prayed for you that your faith may not fail. And when
> you have turned again, strengthen your brothers.
> (Luke 22:31–32 ESV)

These verses from the Gospel of Luke hold so much power and encouragement. While studying the Gospel accounts of the Last

Supper, I came across these verses as if I had heard them for the first time. We see Jesus foretelling Peter's betrayal—talk about a mess! But also, what an encouragement we find here! Jesus, instead of condemning Peter, offered such definitive encouragement that although Peter was going to mess up, and do so quite grandly, he could still turn it around afterward. And when Peter did turn the corner from the mess, Jesus called him to use that experience to strengthen his brothers. Amen! All is not lost, Peter. You might make a mess, but it will be used for good.

When confronted with someone's mess, we don't need to shy away. We can pray for our friend and for her faith to hold fast. Here is what I see that Jesus did in these moments: acknowledge the trial plainly, pray for his friend and the friend's faith, and encourage the friend that the trial is not the end of the story. Let's go through these one at a time.

Acknowledge the Trial Plainly

To acknowledge a trial is no small thing. When friends are facing a trial, one of the greatest gifts we can offer is to name it. When we put words to what they are going through, we demonstrate that we aren't scared off and that we see them right where they are.

Grieving is a good example of this. When someone close to you dies, it can become awkward for all those around you. The most comfort I have found is when a friend shows me she can speak about a trial in plain language. No beating around the bush, no mincing words or avoiding the issue. Freedom can be found in company that calls your mess exactly what it is. I didn't forget about my mess, so a friend speaking plainly about it isn't upsetting. It is actually the opposite. There is a relief found in knowing we can talk openly with our trusted community.

We see Jesus do that here with Peter: "Satan has his eye on you, and you are going to falter." There are no metaphors used, no word pictures. It is just straightforward language. The gift this offers is clear communication. Peter knew without a doubt that someone else was in it with him, fully and knowingly. So name the thing: the death, the divorce, the dirty floors. There is relief and comfort and community found there.

Pray for Your Friend's Faith

In times of trial, there is nothing more comforting than knowing your friends are storming heaven's gates on your behalf. In those prayers, there is solidarity and comfort that is so needed during messy times. I love that Jesus also tells Peter exactly what he has been praying for: that your faith may not fail. What an amazing prayer to be the recipient of.

When you are holding on by a thread, it is easy to feel your faith start to slip through your fingers. Doubts and questions creep in, and you can begin to feel untethered. How comforting, then, is it to know you have friends praying for your faith to hold firm? Sometimes it is hard to know what to pray for your friends when they are in a messy season. Start where Jesus starts: pray for them and for the steadfastness of their faith.

Offer Encouragement

The trial is not the end of the story. Death is not the victor. Neither is any other trial we may face, thanks be to God! When you are facing a mess, though, it is easy not to see beyond your own two feet. That is when we need friends to show us. We need friends to come alongside us and cast a vision of peace and love and victory that we cannot imagine during that time.

When Peter heard that crow the next morning and realized the weight of his denial, I imagine he heard these words in his ear: "When you have turned again, strengthen your brothers." I pray he did. Jesus had already proclaimed victory for Peter. When you turn again. When you come back home. When you clean up the mess. What an amazing reminder that all is not lost. Just because things are messy does not mean the end is here. In fact, just the opposite. When the mess is tidied again, you can use that for good, to strengthen others. We need friends like that. Willingly walking into our mess and proclaiming victory.

There will never be a time in our lives when we are totally mess-free, and the same can be said of our friends. Life is messy, and if we were to wait for the mess-free days to invest in community, we would never get there. Deep community requires getting messy together.

BREAK BREAD TOGETHER

After studying God's Word, we will spend time reflecting, praying, and preparing to take action. Let's have our friendships transformed by our time in the Word!

1. Time to get honest about the shame you carry because of your own mess. How has it caused you to hold back?

2. Are there big messes in your life that feel burdensome to others? Daily messes that are points of embarrassment?

3. Reach out to a friend right now with a prayer request that openly reveals more of your mess.

4. Consider how you can specifically meet a friend in her mess.

Father,

We know we are messy people. Help us to strip away the shame of the enemy. Tear down any walls we have built up as a means of hiding our mess. Remind us that you designed our community, and therefore we can trust them with the untidy corners of our world. Bring that to mind every time we start to hide or hold back. And, Lord, help us look to others with compassion, knowing that we are all messy. Remind us of Jesus and Peter when we are walking in someone else's mess. Let us be friends who declare victory and pray for one another's faith to hold firm. Amen, indeed.

CHAPTER EIGHT

BE TRULY KNOWN

"I am an open book." I can't count how many times I have said that sentence. An open book is a warm, inviting place. An open book offers a world beneath the surface level of the book cover. An open book seems like a great thing to be, doesn't it? But the "open book" status that I boasted about was actually not warm, it wasn't inviting, and it didn't offer a glimpse of what was going on beneath the surface level of my life. Over the years, I had taken on the posture of having a willingness to answer any question about myself with honesty. I wore the title "open book" with pride. A lot of pride.

This willingness to answer any question was coupled with a holding back on how things truly affected me, my heart, soul, faith, and so on. I was transparent and proud of it. My pride came from a sense of comfort in sharing the hard realities. I was never bitter, and therefore I misunderstood my balanced response to my reality as somehow being willing to let others know me. Because we often carry around hard realities in secret or isolation, my willingness to allow others to see what was or had happened led people, myself included, to believe they were getting to know me. However, I was actually unwilling to share the tender truths deep within, the truths that would allow me to be truly known. I was building a transparent wall. Transparency believes in openness, no secrets, but it is a shallow type of openness that keeps us safe and alone behind a glass wall.

While I was still seeking community and muddling through my busy, full, yet lonely life, I was not aware of any of this. I just thought I was an open book. Then I learned of the difference between transparency and vulnerability, and I was cut to the quick. In one particularly thought-provoking post on *Tom Talks*, Thomas Hwang, a pastor and blogger, describes the difference between vulnerability and transparency in this beautiful way:

> "Transparency" means, by definition, the ability to see through something. So when someone's being transparent with you, they're letting you see into their lives. They'll let you know what's going on and even inform you about how they've been feeling. But while people who are transparent will share openly, they do so in a self-conscious, controlled way. In other words, they're presenting a processed, polished version of themselves.
>
> "Vulnerability" though is a little different. When someone's being vulnerable, they're making themselves susceptible to the judgment of others. Vulnerability means they don't just let you know what's going on in their lives— they let you actually see how everything is affecting them. This involves them letting their guard down and relinquishing control. In other words, they're presenting an unprocessed, unpolished version of themselves.

The difference is quite staggering once you consider it. Being forthright did not make me vulnerable.

Vulnerability is a requirement in a Breaking Bread Community. Vulnerability requires a willingness to let the depths be shown, to let the parts of you be known that no one would imagine. Vulnerability builds comfort and trust in your Breaking Bread Community; it allows you to be truly known. And isn't that at the heart of what we are yearning for when we long for community? Our desire to be known is innate in us as humans. The beauty of community is that it allows us to be truly seen and known and loved for who we really are. Sticking with transparency alone, and pride in being an open book, is actually a barrier to authentic community.

Before I was willing to be vulnerable, I had to grapple with many questions that caused turmoil and isolated feelings, even when surrounded by friends. I knew my friends never really knew me, so I would wonder if they actually loved me. After all, I hadn't let them all the way in, so I'd imagine what they would think if they saw all of me. But also, I'd imagine what would happen if I knew I was loved—all of me. It was enough to propel me forward. In one of the hardest parts of my community-building journey, I decided to let myself be truly known.

In *Dance, Stand, Run*, Jess Connolly writes that as a believer, you can't be found out. This was one of the most freeing and revolutionary concepts to wrap my mind around. With Christ, there are no secrets. He knows it all and loves all of you anyway. You can't be found out. There is no sin, no past, no mistake that he doesn't already know about, and yet he loves you, fully and completely. When this truth settled in my soul, I felt truly known, and the freedom it afforded was amazing. If Jesus knows all of me and still chose to die for me, then I get to sit fully in the grace that his death granted. I am fully known and loved, and so are you.

What if we applied the same concept to our community? What if we decided to be so open and vulnerable with our friends that we eliminated the fear of being found out because these people in our lives know us so completely? I think we spend a lot of time whispering to ourselves "if only they really knew," and this holding back is blocking us from being fully known and loved by our friends. This is why praying over this community before you step in is so very important. Because this is a God-designed community, we can have confidence and can trust the most tender parts of ourselves to these people. The fear we have of being seen or "found out" is countered by the fact that God chose these people for you. You can trust them, because you can trust him.

If you happen to be reading this and wondering what on earth I am prattling on about, I want to commend you. But I also want you to know that if you are someone who easily settles into vulnerability, there are things you can do to help your community come alongside you. In every situation, someone has to go first. This may be a great place for you to be that someone. (Now, if this is a struggle for you as it is for me, I am not letting us off the hook, either. Now that we have opened up this can of worms, perhaps we are the ones called to go first in our circles.)

Imagine you are staring down a long zip line through the jungle. As a naturally adventurous person, perhaps you already know all the good stuff awaiting anyone brave enough to take the step off the ledge and seemingly fly through the air. Well, those of us who have never considered such a thing just see a whole lot of risk, and we have no clear vision of the reward. For someone who struggles with vulnerability, going deep with friends is just as scary as rappelling down a jungle zip line. So we could really use a guide—someone who knows the way and has the faith and trust to show us how great this can be.

If you are a person naturally comfortable with vulnerability, encourage us to follow you. Asking specific questions that don't let us off the hook easily is a good start. *How does that make you feel? What are your struggles in this situation or current season?* Wondering questions are great as well. *Have you ever wondered why that is? I wonder what would happen if . . . ?* And lastly, give us space and silence. Be comfortable sitting with the squirming silence. Feeling safe and having time to process almost always results in a more authentic answer.

When answering questions like that, or even just when we're in conversation with our Breaking Bread Communities, I want us to remember that these are the chosen people in our lives. We have already learned they can handle our messes and they want to be here. We get to reveal our true selves to them. So when the conversation slows or there is that one thing you want to say but would naturally hold back on, I want you to push through and say it. In saying it, we step further through the door of authentic community.

I have found more freedom than I ever knew was possible with my people because they know my stuff. They know what drives me crazy, they know what my emotions do when I am exhausted or under stress. They know the challenges my family and marriage have had and how to support me. They know when something is a particular trigger for me because they have seen me at some of my worst times. And, friends, they love me.

Heather and I were both leaders within a ministry for a couple of years as our friendship grew. She was someone I very much looked forward to being with during our ministry meetings. We led our individual small groups simultaneously and shared the struggles and joys that come with such a role. When we were together, we truly connected and enjoyed times full of laughter, prayers, and growing as leaders. Even so, a deep friendship never really blossomed. She would tell you that I intimidated her, and I would tell you that I thought she had enough friends.

But then my friendship with Heather grew to a new level the first time I said the thing I never wanted to say, when I shifted from transparency to vulnerability. It was coming up on May 8, the anniversary of my mother's death. I was really upset that year. I'm not sure if it was the exhaustion of years of grief or more likely the exhaustion of carrying a burden associated with her death, secretly and solely, for several years. As we were sharing prayer requests at our ministry meeting, I simply fell apart. A burden that I had been holding all to myself came bubbling up and out in that moment. I was in the presence of a friend who felt safe. Approaching the anniversary of my mom's passing, I confessed to Heather that what I needed prayer for was for my heart to have peace that I wasn't with my mom when she passed. When I said goodbye to her that morning, I knew it was likely the last day, and now several years later, I couldn't bear the idea that I wasn't there in her final moments. Literally couldn't bear it. The words practically strangled me as they finally came out of my mouth. She died and I wasn't there, and I regret it so much it haunts me.

I had justified this in every way possible, all with valid reasons. I knew, in my head, every rationale offered was true and right, and even that my mom herself would not have wanted me tortured like this, and yet it never felt settled in my heart. I felt shame and embarrassment, I had let myself down, I feared I had let my mom and family down, and I had been carrying around this very weighty silent burden for several years. For the first time ever, I was able to articulate the biggest burden I had held and let myself be seen, not as the grieving daughter but as the one who felt broken herself. My sweet friend prayed over me and hugged me and cried with me. She never judged or justified. She simply saw me and stepped into that sad place and sat there with me. It was the binding moment of our friendship.

Since that particular May 8, all other May 8ths have felt much more peaceful. Imagine if I were still carrying that burden in secret. Imagine if I had missed out on the depth of friendship offered by allowing myself to be truly seen and known and loved. It took a millisecond of bravery to gain a lifetime of deep friendship.

MEET ME AT THE TABLE

In the following passage, we see Jesus sharing deep truths about himself. If we need someone to go first, it doesn't get better than Jesus. He shows us that we can share shocking, bold things with our community. We can trust them with it.

> Jesus answered, "I am the way and the truth and the life. No one comes to the Father except through me. If you really know me, you will know my Father as well. From now on, you do know him and have seen him." (John 14:6–7)

John 14:6 is one of the most quoted pieces of Scripture about Jesus. Surely many of us can recite this one by heart. We know it as such a foundational aspect of our faith that the shocking nature of the statement is sometimes lost on us. It is good to look for the transformational in the familiar, and in this verse, we find both.

As we once again return to the beautiful humanness of this night, let's imagine what it was like to be a friend of Jesus in the Upper Room, as he made an otherworldly statement about who he was and the ramifications of the new covenant. To his friends, he proclaimed that no one gets to the Father *except* through him. I imagine the disciples' first reactions may have been "Come again?"

What Jesus was sharing about his identity was both shocking and unheard of—entirely new. Something like this could easily be misinterpreted or received poorly by the disciples, and yet he shared. When we say the hard thing or expose ourselves to something that can seem unheard of, we are also trusting our friends to handle that information well. Jesus shared this shocking statement with his friends.

What we have to share may feel incredibly tender and raw and vulnerable, and it likely will be, but when we look to Jesus, we see a willingness to share the unfathomable with friends. His willingness and desire to be fully known was demonstrated and satisfied at the Last Supper. As we allow others to truly know us, we will be blessed with deeper, more connected relationships. Just as I experienced a whole new level of friendship and community with Heather for having allowed myself to be truly known, you too can experience such gifts. Let's be vulnerable, not just transparent. Let's let ourselves be truly known, trusting the ones God has called into our lives.

Having vulnerable, intimate friendships not only blesses us and our friends, but it actually points us back to our relationship with God. "That they may all be one, just as you, Father, are in me, and I in you, that they also may be in us, so that the world may believe that you have sent me. The glory that you have given me I have given to them, that they may be one even as we are one" (John 17:21–22 ESV). As Jesus is praying, just before his arrest, he is petitioning the Father and interceding for all believers. His prayer is that we are in the same vulnerable, intimate relationship with God that Jesus has and that we experience the same among our community.

When Jesus announced, "No one comes to the Father except through me," he was saying no one comes *into relationship* with the Father (*pros ton patera* in Greek) apart from him. That same phrase was used in John 1:1, where we are told, "In the beginning was the Word, and the Word was with God" (or, in *relationship* with God, *pros ton theon* in Greek). The Word here is the Logos, Jesus, and again we see the intimate oneness that exists in the relationship between God the Father and Jesus.

Can you see the magnitude of what Jesus was saying in the moments before his betrayal and arrest? For what? For all of us to experience a *pros ton patera*, a relationship with God like he had, and that our oneness with the Father and with Jesus would spill out into vulnerable, intimate friendships in our community. Our friendship with God is grounded in our friendship with Jesus, and we are called to mirror the vulnerable, intimate relationship that Jesus himself had with the Father.

That is a high calling, and I am thankful for the example we have of Jesus and his disciples of being truly known among each other. Trust your friends to see you, all of you. And may that vulnerability point you back to your relationship with Jesus and God the Father.

BREAK BREAD TOGETHER

After studying God's Word, we will spend time reflecting, praying, and preparing to take action. Let's have our friendships transformed by our time in the Word!

1. What are your thoughts on transparency versus vulnerability? Do you find yourself more comfortable with one or the other?

2. What is preventing you from trusting your community?

3. What are you afraid that they may discover about you?

4. As you converse with your friends, practice taking your response from transparent to vulnerable.

Kay Camradina –
2 Cor 1: 4-7   Ps. 55:15
1 Thes 5: 11   2 Cor 12: 9-10
Greg

> Lord,
>
> *We come to you once again thankful for the example of Jesus. As we reflect on the difference between transparency and vulnerability, help us to be vulnerable with those in our community. We trust you, Father, so we know we can trust them. Help us to have strength and courage to be truly known. Father, help us also to be a friend others feel safe with. Grant us your words and patience as our community shares with us. Help us to receive their vulnerability like the precious gift it is. Thank you that we are a people known and seen and loved by you. Let our friendships reflect the same so that we may in turn reflect you. Amen, indeed.*

CHAPTER NINE

EXPECT BETRAYAL, ACCEPT HURT

A while back, I posted a question on Instagram, asking, "What is the biggest challenge you face with friendships?" I expected to hear that people were feeling too busy or unequipped to step into friendship. The largest response I received was the past hurt or betrayal they experienced in friendship. In other words, a hurt from a previous friendship was preventing them from trying friendship again.

This isn't something that is talked about very much. It appears that most of us have experienced painful hurts in our past—one or many that are so painful they are still causing us pain today. If that pain is still having such a profound effect on us, no wonder we aren't willingly opening ourselves up to the potential of another hurt or betrayal. I believe that in an effort to better understand this reality, we need to begin to think of hurt and betrayal as two different friendship wounds. Betrayal and hurt, while both painful, are separate entities. I believe we, and our communities, will benefit from this separation.

Let's start with the big one: betrayal. *Merriam-Webster* defines *betrayal* as "the act of betraying someone or something or the fact of being betrayed" and the "violation of a person's trust or confidence, of a moral standard." Raise your hand if you can relate. (I'm raising both my hands with you.) Here is the bad news—betrayal is to be expected. As we remember that all relationships are comprised of flawed humans, we can see how this makes sense. If we first realize that betrayal is part of what can happen when sin invades our friendships, we can suspend our shock when we encounter it. This is not to suggest that we accept the betrayal and continue on as if nothing is different, but this realization can help us set our expectations in the right place.

The result of suspending our shock is that we can get to the business of dealing with the betrayal. If we remember that we ought to expect betrayal at some point, then we can be prepared for it when it does happen. And deal with it we must. When considering how to participate in a healthy, thriving community, we must fight the urge to shy away or push betrayals under the rug or back into the corners of our heart. Betrayals must be dealt with, but if we deal with them properly, betrayals can be one of our great teachers. Even more promising, betrayals can help move us along into the community God desires for us. But dealing with the betrayal is a tricky thing. The deep pain associated with it makes every conversation that much more challenging. Like you, I have been betrayed. I have dealt with betrayals in a way that was effective and positive and also dealt with betrayals in a way that caused more damage.

I had a friend who caused me quite a bit of stress and anxiety. Looking back, I can see quite clearly the signs of distress in the friendship. The friendship came to a head when she made a comment that was pointed and hurtful, condescending and cutting.

The statement was made not within the heat of an argument, but just as an aside in the middle of a seemingly benign conversation. I remember hearing the words spill out of her mouth and instantly feeling sick to my stomach. Her comment was intended to belittle and hurt, and it did exactly that. I knew in that moment we were done. I literally stood up and said, "Um, I have to go," and then I walked out her door and out of the friendship.

Now you may be reading this and cheering me on, but there was no victory here. I was deeply hurt and betrayed by her words to the point where I no longer felt safe with her. So I left. Here is what I didn't do: I never articulated the betrayal. I never offered any exchange or acknowledgment of what happened. Instead, I simply slunk away. What seemed like an act of self-preservation actually caused more damage to myself and my outlook on friendships and community. I questioned, for years, that final exchange. It's not that I was missing vindication; it is simply that I was missing closure. In the absence of closure, I was left swirling in a sea of doubts and unsettledness.

Another friendship that ended in betrayal had a similar dissolution. I heard cutting words that illuminated how very much a person I had trusted was not "for me." The words showed an ugliness and selfishness that I was startled and unsettled to realize had again shaken me. But this time I knew what to do, or rather what not to do. I was able to calmly call the exchange what it was. I wasn't shocked to find myself again facing betrayal, because betrayal is possible when in relationship. I left that conversation sad at the place our friendship had landed but with clarity that comes from being able to recognize and verbalize betrayal. Subsequently, I had closure and a far greater measure of peace than I had in the same position previously.

While betrayal is to be expected, it is by no means the norm. What most of us face most often is hurt. And hurts are to be accepted. My stories of betrayals both concluded with the end of a friendship. With betrayal, there is often a break in relationship, so this makes sense. We are not called to take this position with hurts. Hurts are painful, yes, but they are surmountable. Hurts are the cost of doing life together with other flawed humans. Accepting hurt looks like offering grace and mercy, talking through uncomfortable things rather than severing ties; it looks like sticking together.

One particular hurt that effects friendship is the hurt of the disappearing friend. This can be a confusing and disorienting experience. For seemingly no reason, a friend just drifts away. Settling that relationship with the other person may or not be possible. If you have reached out and not received a response or acknowledgment, what do you do? I have found the best answer is to start again with prayer. Prayer will eventually offer discernment about whether you are to pursue the friendship further or accept the distance. Either way, there is work that must be done to handle the hurt well. By acknowledging the hurt that exists, even if it is with God alone, you will find healing and a path forward. I've had friends who painfully slipped away, and the result was acceptance. I have had other times when God clearly told me to stay with the friendship. The result was accepting the shift in our relationship, but not a severed tie. Both instances were painful, but both instances also offered healing for me personally and, therefore, peace.

As friends, even in beautiful Breaking Bread Communities, we aren't always going to get it right. We will get hurt and cause hurt. We cannot allow this reality to prevent us from stepping deeper still into community that we were designed for. The most life-giving thing you can realize is that you can have a hurt within a friendship, address it well, and then continue on to have a friendship stronger than it was before. When we discern between hurt and betrayal and respond accordingly, we build Breaking Bread Communities that can last.

MEET ME AT THE TABLE

As we are in practice of doing, let's look to Jesus as our example and see how he handles both betrayal and hurt.

> "I am telling you now before it happens, so that when it does happen you will believe that I am who I am. Very truly I tell you, whoever accepts anyone I send accepts me; and whoever accepts me accepts the one who sent me." After he had said this, Jesus was troubled in spirit and testified, "Very truly I tell you, one of you is going to betray me." (John 13:19–21)

If we needed any clarification that this evening of the Last Supper offers a road map for navigating and nurturing community, in real terms, we need look no further. In John 13:21, we hear Jesus say, quite plainly, that a betrayal is coming. As we picture the group of friends, gathered around the table and enjoying their supper, it is jarring to hear the warning of betrayal spoken so plainly. And yet we learn betrayal is to be expected. The betrayal and hurt on display that night are real-world, present-day community issues, and the Last Supper offers us very specific guidance for dealing with them in our lives today.

Jesus called out the impending betrayal calmly, then . . . moved on with his night. This revelation could have brought an immediate shift to the evening, perhaps bringing the celebration to a halt. It seems reasonable to stop the community time when it is shared that one of his friends is going to betray. But that is not what Jesus did. Jesus called it and then continued on.

How often do we miss the opportunity to do the same? Rather than call it and continue on, I have a tendency to stay and perseverate. I have a tendency to stay stuck in angst and upset. I have a tendency to retreat or cancel. Jesus shows us that it is appropriate to call out what is (or in this case, will be) happening. But he also shows us that it is good and right to move on. *If* we allow the betrayal to stop us in our tracks, frozen and unmoving, what happens? Community in our life would cease, lessons could not be learned. We would stay stuck wallowing in self-pity, anger, and frustration, and then the enemy would win. Imagine if, after Jesus's declaration of the betrayal to come, the evening had ceased. Look at all that would have been lost!

Betrayals, while stinging, are to be named and then released. In so doing, Christ and community are still the victor.

> His disciples stared at one another, at a loss to know which of them he meant. One of them, the disciple whom Jesus loved, was reclining next to him. Simon Peter motioned to this disciple and said, "Ask him which one he means." (John 13:22–24)

While we know that Judas was the betrayer, it is important to note that in the moment, the disciples did not have that knowledge. The scene moves fast, so it is easy to miss. In our previous verses, Christ made the declaration that one of them would betray him, and then verse 22 paints a scene of the disciples looking around the room and wondering which one would be the one. This suggests that at the moment any of them felt it could have been him. All of them were potential betrayers, just as we are all potential betrayers.

Good old Peter is the one who asks what we would all be thinking. . . . Which one of us is it going to be? This reminder is cutting. As we can easily judge the betrayer, let us all remember that in an instant, we can all take on that role. There will be opportunities placed in front of you that will allow you to be a betrayer. We are called to be aware of that capability within ourselves so that we can steward our friendships well and be on guard, rejecting any opportunity to betray others.

Judas has come to be known as the ultimate symbol of betrayal. You may have heard the phrase "He is such a Judas!" used when describing a friend who has betrayed or backstabbed. What is important to note is that there has never been, nor will there ever be, a betrayal to equal Judas's betrayal. Jesus Christ is a singular entity, meaning there is none like him. Consequently, the one who betrays him is uniquely singular. Our deepest betrayals will be painful, yes, but they will not compare to this ultimate betrayal. As we continue to look at the examples of the Last Supper, let's remember that any betrayal we may fall victim to will never be comparable.

Let's instead be friends who value community so much that we honor it by handling betrayal well. Let's call it what it is and continue on in our pursuit of community.

> "You will all fall away," Jesus told them, "for it is written: 'I will strike the shepherd, and the sheep will be scattered.' But after I have risen, I will go ahead of you into Galilee."
>
> Peter declared, "Even if all fall away, I will not."
>
> "Truly I tell you," Jesus answered, "today—yes, tonight—before the rooster crows twice you yourself will disown me three times."
>
> But Peter insisted emphatically, "Even if I have to die with you, I will never disown you." And all the others said the same. (Mark 14:27–31)

This is where we see Christ's willing acceptance of hurt from a friend and the yearning for restoration. You may not immediately think of restoration and acceptance when you read this passage. In this passage, we see the foretelling of the scattering of the disciples and the denial of Peter. How incredibly hurtful to know your community will abandon you; the ones you love are going to let you down. That is what Jesus demonstrates here. However, amid the denial and the harm, amid the hurt of being disowned by your own, it's there for us to see and as an example for us to follow.

In Mark 14:27, Jesus himself said the hurt and harm were coming and ought to be accepted. Jesus quoted Scripture by reminding the disciples it had been written that when the shepherd is struck, the sheep will scatter (Zech. 13:7). He knew it was coming and had already accepted it. In this moment, we are reminded that community and friendship will come with hurt. In other words, we are going to disappoint one another, we are going to say things that are misconstrued or misunderstood, and those things are going to ruffle feathers. We are going to be snarky or short or reactive when we are called to extend grace. When in community, we are going to get hurt.

Don't go running for the hills because I've broken the bad news to you. The hurts we will experience are manageable and will ultimately lead us closer to each other. Restoration. The guarantee of hurts amid community is hard to accept. When we take into account that hurt from a friend is the very reason many of us are unwilling to step back into community, it is especially hard. That is why this passage is so important. Tucked right into the middle of Jesus telling the disciples that they were all going to fall away, and Peter hearing of his imminent denials, was a promise that Jesus would go before them. Amid the hurts, Jesus rose and showed the way.

Don't miss Mark 14:28.

After speaking of the hurts that were imminent, Christ immediately told them that he was going to rise (*amen!*) and that he would go before them. Christ wasn't giving up on them. Christ wasn't saying to them, "You are going to turn your back on me, and I am done." He was saying the opposite, in fact.

Jesus responded to the disciples by pointing them to what was to come. Jesus described when they would be restored. When we experience a hurt from a friend, what a wonderful example for us to follow. We too have the opportunity to pursue restoration. What is required for us to look to the future of the friendship? How can we allow a way for us to move forward? These are great questions to ask ourselves when we have been hurt.

If Jesus's desire is restoration within his community and the kingdom, then we can replicate that within our own community. Hurts are to be accepted to make way for restoration. When examining hurts within community, we also need to stop and look at our pal Peter as he refused to consider that he would be the one to turn his back on Jesus. Despite the very specific warning issued in Mark 14:30, Peter insisted he would sooner die than disavow Jesus. He couldn't imagine that he would be the one to deny Jesus, to do wrong by him. Peter was so confident because he loved Jesus so much. And yet, his humanity and ability to cause hurt crept in. As we know, he did what hours before was unimaginable to him and disowned Jesus multiple times.

It is easy to assume we will not be the one causing harm because, after all, we love our friends and community and would never want to cause them harm. Not I, Lord, not me. But just like Peter, we are often the cause of pain. If any one of us could be a betrayer, then for sure we could be the one to cause a hurt. This is not a question of if, but when. Emphatically insisting that we would never hurt those we love is just as foolish as what Peter said to Jesus that night.

To continue to edify our communities, we must be real that we are often the ones who cause the pain. When we realize we are the one who made a misstep, we can make it right. Restoration is what we are after. The way to restoration is by acknowledging, accepting, and apologizing. When we are the one causing harm, we need to acknowledge and apologize.

If you know anything about the enneagram, you know that an eight, under stress, is not at all a pretty thing. I, being an eight, a challenger, can attest to this. My sharp tongue has gotten me into plenty of trouble in relationships and friendships. My friend Amy has wonderfully, or foolishly, entered into ministry with me and has felt the sting of my biting, snarky tongue, especially when I am under stress. Our friendship and partnership have been a tremendous gift to me. I have learned that when my tongue gets sharp and my patience runs low, I am more apt to say something unkind. It may not be the words I say but a harsh and hurtful tone. As I have continually leaned into this friendship, I am realizing that those little moments of sharpness could easily chip away at our unity as friends. They are small, some may say insignificant, and yet they matter.

I have found that if I am quick to acknowledge the snarky tone or stinging comment and then quick to apologize, the air is clear, unity is intact, and our friendship is better for my having been honest about what I did. Now, this isn't a free pass for me to act like a jerk, and in fact I have discovered that as I become more self-aware, I have fewer of these moments requiring apologies. It's a win-win. I do wonder what our friendship would look like without the bit of self-awareness I have been able to muster. Would expectations continue to be lowered? Would Amy naturally raise her guard? Thankfully, we have found ourselves in the opposite position—more aware, more forgiving, and closer than we have ever been.

BREAK BREAD TOGETHER

After studying God's Word, we will spend time reflecting, praying, and preparing to take action. Let's have our friendships transformed by our time in the Word!

1. Remember a time you were betrayed and a time you were hurt. Can you see the difference?

2. How did you respond to the situations? How would the responses differ if you were modeling what Christ showed us at the Last Supper?

3. Consider a recent hurt; perhaps you were the cause of the hurt, or perhaps you were the one affected. How can you address it with your friend in a way that allows for restoration?

Father,

When we see how Jesus handled both deep betrayal and the hurts of living with friends, we see how important it is to handle them well. So, Lord, show us the way. Help us continually seek out your example, focusing on restoration and unity in our community. Help us discern if there are relationships we must let go of and for us to do that with peace. Help us be quick to acknowledge hurts we have caused and to offer heartfelt apologies that bring us closer together. You are a God of restoration, and for that we are so thankful. Help us to be people of restoration as well. Amen, indeed.

CHAPTER TEN

SHARE
BIBLICAL WISDOM

I will be the first to admit that I love solving problems. If you need a recommendation, I am your girl—never without opinion or resources. I enjoy sharing great information with my friends: a new recipe, a great social media account, a new book. Especially today, there is information available everywhere: books, TED Talks, YouTube, Instagram, podcasts—in this world it seems we have more resources than ever before. It makes it easy to find and share tidbits with friends, and sharing valuable information oftentimes acts as a way of forming connections with each other.

In a Breaking Bread Community, we want more than information; we want wisdom. Where knowledge is about facts or ideas, wisdom offers the ability to discern and judge what is true. That's not to say that we don't get to share our favorite tidbits of information, but we are not called to stop there. If sharing the latest online resource helps us form connections, how much more will sharing true wisdom bind us together? When it comes to wisdom, we need Scripture! Scripture provides unparalleled wisdom and discernment.

When a friend comes to you seeking advice, you will want to be a conduit of wisdom. When a friend wants to know your opinion on a challenge with her kids, you will want to be grounded in Scripture. When a friend is facing a hardship, you will want to have great discernment. Biblical wisdom provides that. In the absence of biblically based wisdom, we are often left filling a void with our own experiences and translating that into action for someone else. While we can learn a lot from each other's experiences, they are not a universal truth. The Word of God, however, is unchanged and unchanging, offering wisdom that we can confidently share with our friends.

Of course, to be able to share with our friends, we need to be familiar with Scripture ourselves. If we agree there is nothing comparable to Scripture, then we must all be spending time with this ultimate source of wisdom and discernment that we have access to. Therefore, the first step in being able to share biblical wisdom is getting into the Word yourself. If you are someone who does not have Bible reading as part of your daily practice, I implore you to give it a try. The Bible blows me away every time I sit with it. If you are a seasoned Bible reader, let me simply encourage you to keep going. New and amazing things, about God and his character, his call on your life, and your salvation through Jesus, will continue to be revealed to you. It will bless you and change you and equip you to bless your friends.

As you spend time in the Word, you will gain the confidence to share biblical wisdom. When your scriptural footing is shaky, it can be very intimidating to share biblical wisdom. I have been in that position before, wanting to offer up something of value that is true and coming up short because I wasn't equipped. Making sure our words are grounded in Scripture can only be done by knowing Scripture ourselves. I love my time in Scripture and have found it so rewarding personally, relationally, communally. The bottom line is we have the honor of instant, easy access to the greatest source of wisdom available, and we serve ourselves and those we love by spending time there.

I have had conversations where I accidentally went along with something out of step because I wasn't aware of where the Bible actually stood on an issue. Because I wasn't rooted in Scripture, I was not able to offer clear and definitive and, most importantly, wise counsel. Our commitment to biblical wisdom is an ongoing part of the Christian walk. We are called to be always seeking. So let's do that. Let's keep seeking the Word, so we are equipped to share a good word with our friends.

As we ensure our words are grounded in Scripture, we need to realize that there are ways to share wisdom that can actually be damaging to our community and our friendships. For example, quoting Scripture as a way to prove a point can be tricky. It can be received as condemning rather than edifying. Within a Breaking Bread Community, we want to share Scripture well, with love and respect for our friends and for the Word. One pitfall to be aware of is plucking Scripture out of context. A short verse with a stinging tone shared outside of context can be a biting experience. It may even shut down the friend to Scripture at all. Oftentimes when we cherry-pick Scripture, we may intend to be helpful, but without the context the meaning is watered down or even changed.

Philippians 4:13 is a great example of this: "I can do all things through Him who strengthens me" (NASB). This verse is often used as a "You can do it!" battle cry. But when a friend is in a tough situation or is struggling, a kick in the pants may not be what is needed. Plus, look at what happens when we take a moment to read the preceding verse. Paul writes, "I have learned the secret of being content in any and every situation, whether well fed or hungry, whether living in plenty or in want." So Philippians 4:13 is not a you-can-do-everything motivational speech but is actually a declaration of contentment within hard circumstances. Context is everything.

Another pitfall is to use the "go-to" verse. Scripture is majestic and there are no "easy" verses within that context, but if you hang around believers for a little bit, you may hear the same few verses used as an answer for tough circumstances. Romans 8:28 comes to mind: "And we know that in all things God works for the good of those who love him, who have been called according to his purpose." I have heard Romans 8:28 many times as a quick Scriptural response to something that is going on in my life. When such verses are used often and without thought, we can become numb to them. What is usually delivered as an attempt to soothe is often received as a mere platitude. What lacks a thoughtful response can also lack comfort. By quickly sharing a verse that is often used, we are missing the opportunity to share wisdom and comfort designed specifically for that person and that situation.

What if when we have a friend in pain or grieving, we first prayed about what God wants us to share with that person? He will likely direct you to something you would never imagine, something far more soothing to your hurting friend. The same can be said for an encouraging Scripture. If we take a moment to seek God's wisdom first, we are better able to share biblical wisdom with our friends.

One morning I received a text from a friend saying that I was heavy on her heart and she wanted to pray for me and encourage me. She asked if I had any requests. As I was in a season of starting a new ministry, as well as an intense writing time, her text was a welcome encouragement in and of itself. After I shared what I was struggling with, she went off to pray, and then she shared another good word of encouragement. She prefaced it by saying that what she was about to share felt off to her, but she was trusting that I would know what to do with it. Then she implored me to say no to every good thing being presented to me that was in conflict of my time, unless it was for those two specifics—my new ministry and my writing.

Let me tell you, that was *exactly* what I needed to hear. How much easier would it have been for her to say, "You go, girl! Keep working hard and I will be praying for strength." A quick Scripture verse, maybe even Philippians 4:13, would have wrapped it up with a bow, and the real words I needed to hear would never have been said. I am so thankful for her wisdom in knowing to stop and ask God before she shared her encouragement with me. Her gentle admonishment was the exact encouragement I needed.

Community works best when we are doing this whole community thing not just *as* Jesus did but *with* Jesus. A very impactful way to do this is to study the Bible in community. If you want to experience the community-building power of sharing Biblical wisdom, there is nothing quite like studying the Bible together. I have done this many ways: in person, weekly, monthly, over text daily, over video chats weekly—there are countless ways of structuring a group Bible study. I have learned that the method of gathering doesn't matter so much as the doing. It can be as simple as a group of friends reading the same Scripture and sharing thoughts and reflections or as involved as a full-on study program.

There is something that happens when we get into Scripture together. There is an openness and connectedness that occurs. As I have shared in studies with friends, I have learned so much more about them, been blessed by their questions, and been encouraged by their prayers, all through studying Scripture. When a friend replies to a reading by sharing how it spoke to an exact struggle she has, it is so tender. When a friend shares how Scripture was particularly encouraging to her heart, you feel honored to be a part of it.

Years ago I found myself, a first-time mom, grieving the recent passing of my own mother and quite lonely. I had attended playgroups, MOPS groups, and Kindermusik classes, seeking connection for myself in this new stage of life. I was desperate for intelligent conversation and empathy and wisdom. I finally found all of those at a group Bible study. This was my first glimpse into what studying the Bible within a community can do. I looked forward to the conversation and the teaching. The very nature of Scripture is one that causes us to reflect and to apply. Scripture allows us to wonder and contemplate in a way that nothing else does. Spending time with that group of ladies showed me how deep and real conversations and connections can be when we study the Word in community.

By spending time in Scripture, you will be able to step into your friends' lives and share what God is teaching you with assurance. Sharing biblical wisdom can often look like sharing what you are learning while you are learning it. My faith has been strengthened by hearing from my friends while God is revealing something to them through their time in the Bible. By sharing our knowledge and insight, as well as how God is revealing himself to us, we learn about each other in a unique way. When I hear from a friend that she is being continually called back to 1 Corinthians and what God is showing her about wisdom and humility, I am doubly blessed. I'm blessed by knowing more about where she is in her heart and blessed by being challenged alongside her to consider what God is revealing. We then have a connection that didn't exist before her sharing. Yet another blessing!

The connection comes from the time spent in the Word and sharing about how God is moving in your life. So many of the good things we have already learned from the Last Supper, inviting, holding space, gathering, and being vulnerable, all naturally occur within the context of studying God's Word together.

MEET ME AT THE TABLE

Have you ever had a shaky moment within your faith? A moment where you think: Can this all really be true? I have. What I learned is that there is a clarity to be found when we know all of Scripture.

> For I tell you that this Scripture must be fulfilled in me:
> "And he was numbered with the transgressors." For what
> is written about me has its fulfillment. (Luke 22:37 ESV)

The Old Testament points to Jesus in a truly prophetic way. In fact, prophecy and fulfillment has become one of my favorite Bible study topics.

A few years ago, I did a Lenten study with She Reads Truth that focused on the book of Isaiah, and spending that much time in Isaiah just blew me away. The book of Isaiah is rich with prophecies that are fulfilled by Jesus. Do you know the odds of the Old Testament prophecies being fulfilled in a single person? The odds of one person fulfilling eight prophecies: one in one hundred quadrillion; the chance of one person fulfilling forty-eight prophecies: one in 10 to the 157th power. And yet Jesus fulfilled over three hundred prophecies! As I spent focused time reflecting on the prophecies fulfilled, I was brimming with a firm sense of assurance in my faith. Clarity. The one the world had waited for had come and was indeed Jesus. Thanks be to God.

The value in knowing these prophecies and seeing the fulfillment in them cannot be downplayed. I find the prophecies and Christ's fulfillment of them to be one of the single most reassuring aspects of the Bible for when your faith feels shaky. They are undeniable and breathtaking. Here at the Last Supper, we see Christ point out the value of them when he said, "For what is written about me has its fulfillment" (Luke 22:37 ESV). He was affirming the validity of those old prophecies and saying he was the one to be the fulfillment. I am not suggesting Jesus's faith was shaky at this point—quite the opposite, actually. Knowing what was prophesized offered him unshakeable certainty.

That certainty is something we can have as well. The clarity we gain when reflecting on the prophecies and their fulfillment in Jesus is demonstrated by Christ himself at the Last Supper. He said, "For I tell you that this Scripture *must* be fulfilled in me" (Luke 22:37 ESV; emphasis added). Jesus knew what had to happen. In an amazing display, he was fulfilling prophecy at the Last Supper while also acknowledging the importance of the prophecy. Jesus knew what he was doing and ensured his friends did as well. He was grounded. That assured grounding comes from knowing the Word, and the only way to know the Word is to read the Word.

> "You will all fall away," Jesus told them, "for it is written:
> 'I will strike the shepherd, and the sheep will be
> scattered.'" (Mark 14:27)

This is one of several times throughout the evening that Jesus demonstrated his knowledge of Scripture. In fact, we have already looked at this piece of Scripture ourselves when reflecting on hurts in Chapter Nine. As a reminder, Mark 14:27 shows Jesus quoting Zechariah 13:7 verbatim: "Strike the shepherd, and the sheep will be scattered." Jesus was addressing the disciples and the fact that they would all turn away from him. If ever there was a misstep, this was one for certain. And this particular misstep was prophesied in Scripture. Jesus used his knowledge of Scripture to frame his discussion with his friends, essentially saying to them that they were headed in the wrong direction. Because he knew the Scripture, Jesus also knew, fully, what God was asking of him. Because Jesus knew this truth, he could comfort and direct his friends with confidence and in a manner that aligned with Scripture.

Wouldn't it have been easier or perhaps more comforting, in the moment, to suggest to the disciples, and Peter in particular, that perhaps they would not turn their backs? Imagine Jesus saying to his friends, I know what Scripture says, but maybe you won't actually go down that road. I know what Scripture says, but maybe it won't be that bad. Taking that position may have made that conversation easier, but it would not have been biblically founded. Instead, Jesus pointed back to what is true, the living Word of God, and reminded his friends that they could count on the solid counsel found there.

We can use our knowledge of Scripture in the same way to counsel our friends, remembering that these are the people God has entrusted to us and us to them. Even still, it is deceptively easy to excuse a sin or a wrongdoing of a friend. It's easy to say, "Maybe you won't go down that road," when we see them taking a misstep. While we think softening the blow may make it easier, we actually run the risk of minimizing something we are called to speak to. Where Scripture is definitive, we must also be definitive. Therefore we must, as Jesus did, have knowledge of Scripture.

BREAK BREAD TOGETHER

After studying God's Word, we will spend time reflecting, praying, and preparing to take action. Let's have our friendships transformed by our time in the Word!

1. How comfortable are you discussing Scripture?

2. How comfortable are you quoting Scripture?

3. What can you do to increase your comfort level in discussing? Quoting?

4. How can you specifically step into the Word with friends? Invite a few friends to study God's Word together.

Scripture gives us unparalleled wisdom —
Have discernment — Wisdom
1 Peter 3:15
Debate —

Father,

Thank you for your living Word. Thank you that it never changes and always is available to us. As we desire to share wisdom with the help of our communities, point us to the true source of wisdom, your Word. Lord, will you draw us close? Will you meet us there each time we open our Bibles? As we begin to study the Word with our communities, grant us an extra measure of grace as we enjoy the deep level of fellowship that can occur when studying the Word together. We seek you first, Lord; be with us. Amen, indeed.

CHAPTER ELEVEN

SPEAK BOLDLY

Our youngest son, Finley, is six years old. His favorite way to connect with people is to ask them questions. He doesn't get involved in the predictable questions, and he has no use for the basic information of age, name, and occupation. Instead, Finley gets right to the heart of the matter. "What is your favorite deadly reptile?" "If you had to be a superhero, who would you be?" "What is your favorite type of vehicle?"

He asks questions with answers that matter to him because he deeply wants to know his people. Finn never asks, "How was your day, Daddy?" or "Are you having a good day?" He wants to know what you are thinking about and whether you are thinking about the same kind of things he thinks about. And so the questions he asks reflect the things that matter to him. I think we can learn a lot from that six-year-old way of thinking.

Rather than asking the mundane questions that result in surface-level answers, what if we decide to have conversations about the important stuff? Within our communities and friendships that we want to nurture, we must choose the meaningful over the meaningless. Floating along the surface of mindless chitchat can leave us feeling empty. Have you ever been there? Had a conversation that felt a bit like a waste of time? I have fallen into that trap even with my closest friends. We spend an hour conversing, and yet there is an emptiness about it. We waste time chatting about nothing, really, and then it's time to go, and everything just feels off. There is a time for lighter conversations, sure, but that is not how you build and maintain the bonds of deep community.

Speaking boldly, having the big conversations, asking the hard questions allows for soul-satisfying conversations and connections that run deep. I'd like more of that, please. My friend Kristen has taught me so much in this way. Kristen always has a great question at the ready. I have learned from her that asking interesting questions demonstrates an interest in the other person. It demonstrates a desire to know something new about your friend, something deeper. Having been the one to receive these kinds of questions, I will say it also communicates so much love and value!

Rephrasing common questions is an easy way to do this. Rather than asking, "How was your day?," you could ask, "What did you do today?" It's a simple change, yet the difference in response is so impactful. "How was your day?" can be answered with a simple "good." But when you ask friends specifically how they spend their time, you will learn what is going on in their world. Taking the same concept even further, imagine starting a conversation off by saying, "I have been thinking a lot about the Prodigal Son lately. Have you considered x?" In other words, get right into it. We all have limited time, and therefore if you are able to sit and chat with your friend over coffee, make it a valuable time.

These are the people you are wanting to go deeper with, so go deep! Fear can play a large part in our holding back. As a practice, pivoting from fluffy conversations to deep conversations can feel strange at first. Will your friends follow along? Will they want to go deep as well? What if you are misunderstood or the pivot is unwelcome? Those fears or hesitations are understandable. I have found that "your people" are yearning to spend valuable time with you. And that time is often spent in conversation. As you begin to put this into practice, you will be amazed at where you have the most impactful conversations . . . school parking lots, soccer fields, grocery stores.

I believe we yearn to dive deep into meaningful, interesting conversations, but it's easy to think that these conversations must be held at special times set aside for deep conversation. I want to challenge that thought. If we remember that God has called us into relationship with these people and that we are called to have an impact on one another, we must seize the time we have, whenever that may be, to have the good conversations and to speak boldly.

Perhaps it is my own desire to be focused or my innate love of list making, but I have even been known to write out a conversation topics list on my phone when I know I am going to get a block of time with a friend. It seems ridiculous, but it's effective. I have found that taking the time to make the list is actually the most effective part of the process. The intentionality is set internally, and the conversations are focused, deeper, and life-giving. In fact, I have often checked my list during time with a friend, only to find that we have already covered most of the topics I had in mind. By making that list, I had already decided I wasn't going to waste time with my friend on frivolous chatter. While I don't think all conversations need to be serious, there is great value in having intentional, meaningful conversations. If it requires a list-making exercise to get yourself focused, go for it! As with most things, the more you do it, the more likely you are to keep doing it.

Speaking boldly also looks like saying the good things that our friends need to hear. We get to be the ones to proclaim goodness and abundance for our friends when they can't see it themselves. We get to shine a light on their strengths and how they can use them. We get to call out the good we see. Speaking boldly is often acknowledging our friends and saying, "I see you." It is one of the very best parts of belonging to a Breaking Bread Community.

My favorite part of any Birthday Club dinner is when we go around the table and share what we admire about the honoree and what we pray for her for the coming year. One by one, we call out the very best of our friend and then cast a vision for her coming year. To look your friend in the eye and tell her what is admirable about her is a holy thing. I believe it is the thing that cemented my little community together in deep ways.

As you continue to get to know your friends on a deeper level, there will be so much you admire about them. So often we keep these things to ourselves and miss out on the opportunity to speak boldly over our friends. I understand that it can feel awkward. It can be awkward to say all these compliments, and it is for sure awkward to receive. But press into it because it is so valuable. When you verbalize how special someone is, how she has changed you, and the goodness you see in her, you are honoring her and your friendship.

The first time we met as the Birthday Club, I surprised my friends by instituting our roundtable of admiration. Everyone was more than willing to participate . . . except the guest of honor. It is a hard and uncomfortable thing to sit and receive such sweet words. But a beautiful softening happens as we work our way around the table. You can see the words begin to sink in and the guest of honor fully receive them. We are several years in to the Birthday Club, and almost every get-together is met with groans of objection from whomever is being honored. And yet again, we press in. We speak bold words and our friends are blessed.

Our friends need our encouragement, and God has placed us in a position to uniquely encourage and embolden them.

MEET ME AT THE TABLE

In the following passage, we are reminded that Jesus knew the power of words spoken over his friends and intentionally used his words at the Last Supper to equip the disciples for later. In the previous twenty or so verses, Jesus reminded the disciples of their love and friendship and then warned them of persecution that would come because of their relationship to him. He knew the disciples' faith would be tested, that struggles awaited. So he directed them to remember the bold words spoken over them.

> I have told you this, so that when their time comes you
> will remember that I warned you about them. I did not
> tell you this from the beginning because I was with you.
> (John 16:4)

We too have struggles awaiting us, and surely our faith will be tested. When our friends have already spoken boldly over us, when they have already claimed victory for us, we too can remember their words. The words spoken over us will strengthen and encourage us. When we are generous with our words to our friends, we are equipping them for their future.

At least two years before I typed my first word for a book, my friend Amy boldly spoke over me. "You are going to write a book," she said. I brushed it aside. I said maybe a blog post or a workbook, but a book? Not me. I am not capable of that, nor equipped for it.

But my friend listened to the prompting in her heart and spoke it aloud over me. "A book." Writing a book is not for the weak of heart. It is a marathon, when I prefer a sprint. It requires discipline and so much work that no one will ever see. There have been many times when I have wanted to quit or felt utterly ill-suited to the calling. Yet I remembered the words of my friend, boldly shared, in the middle of a thrift shop: "A book." Those words have been to me exactly as Jesus said, given so that when the time came, I would remember.

The boldness of those words is what was ultimately so comforting. They were spoken well before I was in the project. Amy had no way to know for certain that this is where I was headed, yet she was faithful in sharing them. And through her faithfulness, I have been blessed every time I was ready to quit or doubted the calling or felt frustrated. Imagine if she had not been so bold?

I catch my breath when I think of times that I stepped back from speaking boldly. What opportunities have I missed to step in line with the Spirit and equip someone? In a life filled with many losses, I have learned the value in saying the words while we can. This gift extends beyond your family. When prompted, speak up. It is not your job to know how your words will be used, but the words you share will surely be used to encourage your community.

When our friendships have a history of care and love and honest conversations, it makes another kind of "bold speak" much easier. As a Breaking Bread Community, we have the responsibility, and the honor, of having the hard conversations, too. With our friends, we are sometimes to call out the hard places we see them stuck—opportunities to extend grace that they missed, relationship-damaging decisions they are making. When our friendships are rich and rooted in truth, these hard conversations become sweet and sanctifying rather than condemning and judgmental.

As we have already established, I do not like being told what to do. So you can imagine how much I like being told that what I am doing is wrong. The friends now around me are able to point out where I might be missing the mark. These conversations are approached with grace and, yes, boldness. They are effective conversations because I am blessed by friends who do not shirk away from the hard things. When I am casting unnecessary judgment or holding too tight to things that I cannot and should not control, they see it and call me to live life a different way, more in step with my faith.

My marriage is better for these conversations. My relationships are better for these conversations. I am a better mom and friend and minister of the gospel for these conversations. Those encouraging conversations that could be hard are well-received because of the history of our relationship. When there is history filled with words of affirmation and with seeing all that is good and true in one another, there is confidence that even the hard conversations are coming from that place of love and goodness.

It's always helpful to remember that receiving these conversations is much easier than delivering the conversations. So if you are receiving bold words from your friends, do so with grace, knowing they love you enough to speak boldly. And if you are called to speak boldly in this manner to your friends, go filled with grace. Remember that we are called to equip rather than condemn our friends. If we approach the conversation in a way that communicates love and belief in them, and God's call on their life, it will be a beautiful conversation.

I have been so honored to be called into that role and have found these conversations to be the most Spirit-filled. I have sat across from more than one friend and heard hard things that I had to speak boldly about. Because I love them, I knew I had to say something. Text messages that had gone too far, relationships out of place, marriages awry—these are things that required me to get out of my comfort zone and offer a definite redirection for them and their lives. What could have been very condemning conversations were actually full of love and encouragement and belief in who they are and the life God has for them. Every time I have found myself in one of those conversations, if I handled it from a place of encouragement, I reached the end of it closer and more connected to that friend than I was before.

Bold words, both heard and spoken, make me feel loved, encouraged, and not alone. Speaking boldly, among friends, is a tremendous gift.

BREAK BREAD TOGETHER

After studying God's Word, we will spend time reflecting, praying, and preparing to take action. Let's have our friendships transformed by our time in the Word!

1. Are you frustrated by fluffy conversation?

2. Brainstorm some bold questions to take your conversations deeper.

3. Reflect on a time when a friend spoke boldly over you. How did you feel? Did you receive it well? Similar to service, we need to receive these beautiful, bold words from our friends well.

4. What can you remind yourself of when you have the hard conversations, so you don't shy away from them?

5. How can you receive the hard things from your friends well?

God,

Thank you for Jesus being a friend who speaks boldly. Help us to be the same. Tune our hearts to be in line with the promptings of the Spirit. Help us to cast aside fear or self-awareness as we speak of the goodness of our friends to them. Let us trust that you will use those words to equip our friends for the future. Lord, when we are together, help us not to waste time on the surface but to dive deep with the ones you have set aside for us. And when the bold words come with a bit of correction for us to consider, let us do so humbly, remembering these are the people you have placed in our lives to be an influence. Let us listen to our friends and believe them when they speak boldly over us, for good and for better. Amen, indeed.

Potential Questions to Spark
Good Conversations —

What did Jesus do for you?
What did you do today?
What can I pray for you?

✱ Titus 2:7-8   Eph 5: 8-11
2 Timothy 4:5   Be the Light
Colossians 3:16   Pray for
✱ 2 Tim 3:16   Audrey
Prov 19:20
      12:1
Prov 15:31-33
      12:15

CHAPTER TWELVE

CELEBRATE TOGETHER

Celebrating is a big part of my life. I was in the event planning industry for over ten years, and while celebrating was my vocation, it was and still is something I am called to do in all aspects of my life. I am constantly on the hunt for things or people to celebrate. My favorite definition of *celebrate* can be found in *Merriam-Webster*: "to mark something by festivities or other deviation from routine." Celebrating causes us to stop and notice. It causes us to mark a moment in time as important. When we are looking to grow roots in community, the call is to celebrate together.

The problem for me arises when life gets complicated or I am facing a hardship; my personal response is to stay rooted in joy and, yes, to celebrate, but to do so while keeping friends at arm's length. This is not good for community. As I worked my way through crisis after crisis for a decade, I stopped celebrating with my friends. When I began noticing the emptiness and yearning for genuine, invested community in my life, I also noticed that I had stopped celebrating with them.

Separating friendships from celebrations doesn't always require a crisis to make us pull away, however. Sometimes the busyness of life, motherhood, and adulthood can be cause enough to stop celebrating or at best stop celebrating with community. The time constraints of our schedules, the limits of our finances, the lie that we have nothing valuable worth celebrating can all cause us to neglect the call to celebrate. Holidays are often reserved for families, and inviting friends into family dynamics can be tricky. Sometimes it is easier to keep celebrations small and the guest list short.

Celebrations are an intimate thing. They often are tied to a milestone or holiday, and it can feel risky to open those up to friends. The beauty of celebrating milestones together is that we are not just sharing our history; we are asking others to actively participate in our history-making moments. Inviting a friend into a celebration is saying, "This matters to me, and I want to experience it with you."

I remember the first time we hosted friends for a major holiday about fifteen years ago. I had placed a lot of pressure on myself to make it a Thanksgiving that would be joyous for all. I called Mom, asking her for any advice on how to make this a success. I had never hosted a holiday before and adding friends, not just family, to the guest list made the stakes feel even higher. I was concerned that our somewhat nontraditional yet traditional-for-us side dishes of roasted root vegetables and veggie lasagna would be too unfamiliar and make our friends uncomfortable. That being said, I was not at all prepared to give up any of the veggies! My mom said something brilliant that has stuck with me to this day: "You are inviting them to your celebration. Let them experience it the way you do it. Think of it as a gift to share it with them. But offer them the same opportunity. Ask what dishes they always have at their Thanksgiving, and let them share with you as well."

Celebrating together is a gift to be shared.

Something as silly as a veggie lasagna can feel vulnerable in that context, but I encourage you to go for it anyway. That Thanksgiving is one I look back on so fondly. We had more food than necessary with side dishes from both families, including root vegetables, veggie lasagna, and also the green bean casserole of our friends' childhoods, plus dessert made up of our family favorite Pumpkin Banana Mousse Tart and our friends' favorite Banana Cream Pie. It was a feast of food, friendship, and gratitude—just what Thanksgiving ought to be.

I remember all of us squeezing into the tiny dining alcove of our log cabin in the Berkshire Mountains. I remember the walk we took before dinner down our country road with the unexpected November sunshine warm enough not to need a coat. I remember lingering at the table and sharing stories and laughter and feeling so utterly and overwhelmingly content. It was a delight! We were carefree and able to enjoy every moment of that holiday celebration. There was a sweetness and intimacy in having friends with us at our holiday table, and it was good.

As I found myself fifteen years later seeking deeper connections and community, I realized that celebrating joy with my family was good, but not enough. We are called to celebrate with friends as well. Without realizing it, I had circled the wagons around my family so tightly that it left no room to celebrate with my community. What had started out as a response to a season of trials had grown into an isolation technique. I had been depriving myself of one of my favorite ways to connect.

The Birthday Club was paramount to my celebrating with friends again as a way to connect with my community. Celebrating birthdays together was, and continues to be, a sweet and beautiful way for us to connect deeper as friends. Birthday Club dinners have a different feel than a typical girls' night out. There is a quality about the gathering that is singular to a celebration: the joy, the jubilation, the anticipation, and the elation at joining together . . . it is all intensified because of the celebration factor. Throughout the night, we are excited to celebrate one of our own, to mark someone as important. The time we spend is richer and more meaningful because we are *celebrating* together. To think that anyone, including myself, has been depriving herself of this act of community is heartbreaking to me. After a few months of celebrating with the Birthday Club, I could see the clear connection between community building and celebration.

Through celebrating birthdays, holidays, and life itself, we draw closer together. There are moments of celebration available to us all the time. If celebrating your birthday with friends doesn't get you excited, consider other moments that you can include your friends. Perhaps host a holiday meal with friends, or celebrate the end of a school year together. You can celebrate a job promotion, a new home, a graduation. You can celebrate Taco Tuesday. If you mark it as something special and deviate from routine, you have yourself a celebration. The point isn't which celebration you are stepping into together, as long as there are moments of celebratory joy within your community.

Oftentimes we don't step into celebration because we do not believe ourselves or our lives worthy of celebrating. We aren't fun enough, special enough, prepared, equipped, ready, or deserving. All lies. Celebration is a gift modeled for us by Jesus, and you are deserving without changing a thing about you or your circumstances. Challenge yourself to consider how celebratory your life is. As you reflect, you may be surprised by how much you hold back on celebrating.

When our youngest, Finley, had just turned four, we had a series of sweet, small celebrations for him during his birthday week—each unique and not overly complicated. The final celebration was a small group of his friends, their siblings, and the moms who comprise the bulk of my Breaking Bread Community. It was a great night full of all the things an old-fashioned party at home should be: crepe paper streamers, balloons, cupcakes, and kids running around. The next morning as I sat down with my coffee and reflected on the celebration, I saw it for the first time—the true connection between friendship and celebrating together.

Have you ever watched your friends sing "Happy Birthday" to one of your children? It brings me to tears every time. Women called into my life and therefore into my family's life are pouring out love and joy and delight at marking a milestone together. After a long season of struggles, heavy burdens, and more than our share of emergencies, I welcomed my friends into celebration with me for the first time in a long time. With that invitation came a levity that had been missing for too long, sweeping through my house and my family like a breath of fresh air.

MEET ME AT THE TABLE

Let's not forget that the Last Supper was a celebration. We tend to get focused on Jesus's teaching or on the events at the table itself, while diminishing the notion that this was a holiday celebration. Jesus himself demonstrated a desire to celebrate together with his friends.

> And he said to them, "I have earnestly desired to eat this Passover with you before I suffer." (Luke 22:15)

This verse, while at first glance a short piece of Scripture, has four key components that require careful study and reflection to glean the fullness of meaning. If we move too quickly, we run the risk of losing out on the depth of the example we see in Christ and will, therefore, lose out on the fullness of application this verse has on our own lives and friendships. We are going to take this one slow and learn all we can about what Jesus says about celebrating with your friends.

"I Have Earnestly Desired"

Here is the phrase that stopped me in my tracks: "I have earnestly desired." Having studied Passover in depth for years, I knew Jesus wanted to celebrate Passover with his disciples, but I always missed the desire, the yearning. This is where a word study proves to be very helpful. Jesus said to the disciples, "I have earnestly desired," or the King James translates it as, "with desire I have desired." This manner of speaking is characteristic in Hebrew as a way of expressing intensity. This phrase comes from the word *epithymia*, which means a longing, and the word *epithymeo*, which means to set the heart upon. What Jesus is saying here is, "With longing I have set my heart upon eating this Passover with you before I suffer." Through understanding the Greek, you get a clearer picture of the intensity of what Jesus is saying.

Celebrating with his friends was so important to Jesus that he literally had set his heart upon it. If Jesus had his heart set on something, then I think we want to pay attention to it. Now, here is the part that makes my research-loving heart get very excited— this is the only time that Jesus articulates a personal desire.

The only time.

Gathering to celebrate with the disciples is the singular thing Jesus voiced a desire for. There is no other instance within the

Bible when Jesus speaks about his desire. No wonder we have a desire for community ourselves!

"To Eat This Passover"

There are debates in commentaries about whether the Last Supper was in fact on Passover or perhaps the day before. Either way, Jesus voiced his desire to celebrate this most special festival, which was a holiday, with his friends. Jesus did not voice an earnest desire to meet or to teach, although both of these occurred at the Last Supper. Jesus voiced an earnest desire to gather and celebrate.

The Passover served as the initial reason for this celebration and gathering of friends. If you are not familiar with it, Passover is a festival celebrating the deliverance of the Israelites from Egyptian slavery. After several attempts to compel Pharaoh to release the Israelites, God sent an angel of death to strike Pharaoh's people. The Israelites, instructed by God through Moses, marked their homes by applying the blood of a spotless lamb to their doorways, thus confirming that they were God's chosen people, and the angel of death passed over their homes. This was the night of Israel's release to freedom and the Exodus story. The Passover festival in Jesus's time was a holy festival set aside to recall this event and to remember God delivering his people. The culmination of the Passover festival was a beautiful, symbolic meal around the table.

Jesus used this celebration to lay out the gospel, first for his friends and then for the world. Jesus flipped the entire meaning of the Passover meal and the Exodus story to point to himself as the true lamb and his sacrifice as the ultimate sacrifice, thus presenting redemption for the entire world. The gospel, the redemption of the world through Jesus, and celebration are intrinsically tied together.

"With You"

There is total clarity in this statement. Luke 22:14 says, "When the hour came, he reclined at table, and the apostles with him" (ESV). Therefore, when Jesus said, "I have earnestly desired to eat this Passover *with you* before I suffer" (Luke 22:15; emphasis added), there is no question who the "you" is. The desire was to gather and celebrate with the disciples, his inner circle, his deep community, his friends.

When I imagine who could have been on the invite list for this dinner, I am humbled to see who Jesus chose. The significance of the time we spend celebrating with friends is made clear to me in this passage. When able to invite anyone, Jesus invited his friends.

"Before I Suffer"

This Passover, Christ knew, signified the time for him to assume the role of the lamb. This was a heavy time. But it is important to note that still there was time to celebrate. We have two lessons to learn here.

First, we see Jesus stepping into celebration while also facing hardship. He knew suffering was imminent, yet he celebrated. Jesus was facing a grueling death, yet he did not pause to wallow. This was no pity party. This was a genuine celebration motivated by the gospel and the redemptive work of Jesus. We too can celebrate amid any circumstance. When we are facing our own hardships, we can continue to step into celebration. How can this be possible? Regardless of our circumstances or the hardships we may be facing, we are empowered to celebrate by Christ himself. When we are in Christ, there is always a reason to celebrate.

Second, we need to remember that the suffering Jesus referred to in the verse was the completion of his work. When Jesus said "before I suffer," he was demonstrating the value of pausing to celebrate even before the race is done. Can you believe it? He was telling us that we, too, can celebrate before things are in the ideal state. How often do we wait to celebrate until the accomplishment is achieved, the crisis is ended, the finish line is crossed, the miracle is realized? When we look at Jesus, we see how to step into celebration, regardless of our circumstances and even before the work is complete.

We are not called to wait on things being perfect to celebrate. Imagine if Jesus had held off on celebrating until his death, and his resurrection had already transpired. What wonderful things we all would have missed from the Last Supper. Thanks be to God there was a different plan. Jesus showed us that we gather and celebrate, and we don't wait for things to be all right to do so. There is much to celebrate even during a trial and before the miracle. Don't wait, friends!

BREAK BREAD TOGETHER

After studying God's Word, we will spend time reflecting, praying, and preparing to take action. Let's have our friendships transformed by our time in the Word!

1. What do you earnestly desire?

2. How often are you celebrating, not just gathering, with friends?

3. How can you celebrate now even in the mess, the busyness, the hardships of life?

4. What can you celebrate with your community? Make it joyous and special!

> Father,
>
> We hear so clearly Jesus's heart in this passage. May we too yearn to celebrate with our friends. Encourage us to find joyous celebration regardless of the hardship or hectic nature of our life today. Help us to value celebration as you do. Help us to create that community cement to bind us together as we gather in celebration. Lay upon our hearts a vision of celebration that we can enjoy with our community. Amen.

CHAPTER THIRTEEN

MAKE A
JOYFUL NOISE

Throughout the Psalms we are commanded to make a joyful noise unto the Lord. We see it in Psalm 66, Psalm 95, Psalm 98, and Psalm 100. "Make a joyful noise to the LORD, all the earth; break forth into joyous song and sing praises!" (Ps. 98:4 ESV). We are reminded of the beauty of bursting forth with song. As a die-hard audiophile, I love these psalms. I have learned the power of music as a means of worship, as a way to manage my mood, and as a way to celebrate. I have different playlists for each season. I have songs that remind me of very specific times in my life. Music can transport me through space and time much the same way food can. Music is powerful.

Enjoying music with your community is another wonderful way to create deeper bonds of friendship. For some of us, this can look like sharing a concert experience or sharing the newest albums from a favorite musician. These are wonderful experiences to share with your friends. I have found, however, that something truly transformative happens when we slow down and sing the hymns together.

One day a bunch of us were in a car together, and after plenty of quality discussion time over a weekend together, we were heading home. As is often the practice, we began discussing what we should listen to. Kristen, the one with the amazing ability to inject deep meaning into everyday moments, said, "Let's sing some hymns first." As we cruised along the Massachusetts Turnpike, we took turns calling out hymns we knew. We pulled out cell phones when we weren't sure of lyrics. We shared memories we had associated with a certain hymn as it came up. My minivan was never filled with such sweet sounds as it was that day.

As with most things, sharing quality music is great, but sharing biblical music is better. It may feel corny or strange or foreign to you, but you never know how you'll feel about it until you try. If you are stuck for a place to start, you could always try the Doxology. It is beautiful and simple and will leave you breathless when you are surrounded by the sweet voices of your community singing.

> Praise God, from whom all blessings flow;
> Praise him, all creatures here below;
> Praise him above, ye heavenly host;
> Praise Father, Son, and Holy Ghost.
> Amen

Another joyful noise for us to consider as we grow our community roots is the sweet sound of prayer. Prayer is a large part of a Breaking Bread Community. It has come up several times already, but let's look at prayer as a way to share a joyful noise with each other while continuing to grow closer together.

If you want to get to know someone, or if you want to truly communicate how valued a person is to you, I have found no better question to ask than "How can I specifically be praying for you?" That exact question will draw out the heart of your friend as she shares what she needs. My friend Amy and I start every morning at six with that very question. Over the years, our hearts have been knit together in the most beautiful way with the asking and answering of that question.

As you begin to use this question within your own community, you will have the opportunity to pray for your friends. But more importantly, you will have the opportunity to pray *over* your friends. A commitment to pray is wonderful. But nothing compares to a friend stopping a conversation and saying, "I want to pray for you right now." This can be done in person, over the phone, or even via text. The comfort found in receiving the actual prayer in writing or verbally simply does not compare to being told, "I'm praying for you."

I have received the most beautiful texts from the prayer warriors in my life. They were rich with detail and assurance in our good God. To have that tangible thing to go back and read has been so encouraging to me as the one receiving the prayer. The first time I received such a text from a praying friend, I remember being taken aback. Our daughter had been going through a very hard situation at school, and I asked a friend who had a soft spot for her to cover her in prayer. Next thing I knew, my phone was going crazy with notifications as a flurry of praise and petition came into my messages. The detail and care expressed in the actual prayer written out versus the "I'll be praying!" comment was tangible.

It was a good lesson for me as a praying friend. I definitely fell into the "I'll be praying for you" camp. As I received these beautifully articulated prayers, I realized that I could bless people in my life the same way. As I began to practice written prayers, what at first felt awkward became much easier and more comfortable. I have begun to love praying for my friends "live." Praying aloud or in written form can feel intimidating, but I encourage you to step into it. Praying over friends is a truly beautiful way to make a joyful noise on their behalf.

MEET ME AT THE TABLE

As was traditional for practicing Jews, Jesus and the disciples ended this important meal by singing a hymn. As I picture this group of men singing, I can't help but recall that minivan full of my friends also singing hymns together. How sweet the sound.

> And when they had sung an hymn, they went out into the mount of Olives. (Matt. 26:30 KJV)

The hymns the men would have been singing are called the Hallel psalms, or praise psalms. In the Jewish tradition, festival meals such as the Passover would have ended by singing Psalms 113 through 118. This series of psalms were prayers, sung in praise. So we see both prayer and song coming together to praise God. When we're wondering what to sing, we too can turn to the hymns; they are our songs of praise.

We don't hear much about this moment of the Last Supper. I find it to be such a tender thing to picture. At the end of this meal, the gospel now laid out before the disciples, they gathered to sing a song of praise. The Hallel psalms, the prayers these men shared, were for certain a joyful noise.

If the idea of praying for your friends leaves you feeling excited but unqualified, we have the most amazing example of intercessory prayer as Jesus spent time with his friends the evening of the Last Supper. We see Jesus pray what is known as the High Priestly

Prayer, his longest recorded prayer, in John 17. The chapter offers so much for us to observe and study as followers of Christ. Jesus looked to heaven and began to pray for himself, for his disciples, and then for all believers. It is a dynamic and beautiful prayer, rich with meaning and far too vast for us to study in its entirety. For our purposes, we are going to focus on John 17:6–19, the section where Jesus prayed specifically for the disciples.

As we observe Jesus intercede on behalf of his friends, let us first remember that when we offer intercessory prayer, whatever it looks like, we are accepting an invitation to be more like Christ. Intercession allows us to be Christlike as we approach the Lord on behalf of our friends. It is an honor and a gift to do so. If we are looking for examples of what to pray on behalf of our friends, or how to pray for them, we see Jesus offer some specific petitions that we can also pray as we intercede for our community. Jesus first declared whose they are and then prayed that they be kept and that they be sanctified.

> I am praying for them. I am not praying for the world but for those whom you have given me, for they are yours. (John 17:9 ESV)

As he began his prayer, Jesus declared that the disciples were a gift to Christ and that they were God's. In other words, Jesus began by affirming whose they were. In so doing, he was also declaring *who* they were. As we pray for our friends, let us remember whose they are: a gift to Christ and belonging to God himself. The belonging that comes from being a daughter of the King is an identity that we get to declare over our friends as we pray for them. Reminding our friends of their identity is such a powerful way to start prayers for them.

While I was with them, I protected them and kept them
safe by that name you gave me. None has been lost
except the one doomed to destruction so that Scripture
would be fulfilled. I am coming to you now, but I say
these things while I am still in the world, so that they
may have the full measure of my joy within them. I
have given them your word and the world has hated
them, for they are not of the world any more than I am
of the world. My prayer is not that you take them out
of the world but that you protect them from the evil
one. They are not of the world, even as I am not of it.
(John 17:12–16)

After praying over their identity, Jesus went on to pray that
they be kept. He prayed that the disciples be kept safe, kept joyful,
and kept in the world but not worldly. Safety, especially from
spiritual attacks, is a super important thing to pray over your
friends. When praying for our friends, we can pray for their protection regardless of whether they seem to be under attack or not,
because they will be, and prayers of intercession are always needed.
Breaking Bread Communities, friendships that reflect Jesus, will
come under attack. The enemy will view you and your friendships
as a threat, and he will retaliate. Pray for your friends to be kept
safe and pray for it often.

Jesus went on to pray that they be kept joyful. In fact, Jesus
petitioned that they experience joy fully and that it reside within
them. This single verse (John 17:13) is sandwiched between the
petition for safety, acknowledging that one has already fallen, and
declaring that the world has hated them. Jesus was crying out for
joy in the middle of the hard things the disciples had faced and
would face. Often, we pray for our friends to get through a hard

situation: survival is the prayer. Yet here we are reminded to pray for them to flourish joyfully, despite the hardships they face. As we pray for our friends, let us pray boldly that they experience the fullness of joy.

Finally, Jesus asked that his friends be kept in the world but to not become worldly. Just, *yes!* Prayers of steadfastness, faith fulness, and a call to live differently can be daily petitions of ours as we intercede on our friends' behalf. In this prayer, we see the reminder of identity and the request for safety come together as Jesus prayed that these friends stay where they were, protected and set apart. The world presses in from all sides, and it is so easy to become of the world as we stay here in the world. We can pray for this specific edification for our friends as we all reflect Christ in our friendships and as we interact with the world.

> Sanctify them by the truth; your word is truth. As you
> sent me into the world, I have sent them into the world.
> For them I sanctify myself, that they too may be truly
> sanctified. (John 17:17–19)

Jesus ended his prayer specifically for the disciples with these final verses as he petitioned for their sanctification. Sanctification is the process by which we grow more like Christ throughout our lives. Jesus prayed that his friends would be sanctified in particular by the Word.

As we studied in Chapter Ten, biblical wisdom is helpful to growing a thriving community. Jesus asked that the truth of the Word would be a means of making them pure, setting them apart for sacred purpose. Jesus then declared that the way to true sanctification came from himself and his own sanctification on the cross. This is a powerful reminder to pray for salvation of those friends who have not yet experienced true saving. We are called to pray for our friends' initial salvation and then for the continued sanctification in their lives as they live, set apart.

Praying for our friends as intercessors allows us to be Christlike in our behavior and encouragement. As we echo his prayers for our friends, we too will be making a joyful noise.

BREAK BREAD TOGETHER

After studying God's Word, we will spend time reflecting, praying, and preparing to take action. Let's have our lives transformed by our time in the Word!

1. What type of music do you enjoy listening to?

2. Considering prayer and singing, which joyful noise most speaks to you?

3. Call or text a friend and ask, "How can I be specifically praying for you?"

4. Respond by praying over that person. This can be via text or in person, but practice stopping what you are doing and specifically praying over someone.

5. Pray for protection over your friends as you continue to reflect the love of Jesus.

"Hallel" Ps. 113:118
Jewish prayer —

> *Father,*
>
> *We are in awe of all that took place at the Last Supper. As we continue to follow your example, guide us. We want to be friends who make a joyful noise. Lead us in song and praise and prayers with our friends and over our friends. Lord, we pray protection over our communities; bind Satan, we pray, and encourage us to be bold friends of prayer and praise. Amen, indeed.*

John 17 - Jesus longest
prayer for His disciples.
* Intercession as Christ the
a- I am praying for Them.
Identity *1. Be Kept. Safe *2. Joyful
*3. In the world but
not worldly.
* Grow more like Christ
through the Word

165

CHAPTER FOURTEEN

GRIEF TURNS TO JOY

As we are committed to doing real life with our Breaking Bread Community, we will inevitably experience grief. Trials and hardships are inevitable. Tragedy will strike, illness may come, someone could move away. As a community, how do you handle that heartbreak? As has been the theme throughout my journey into deep friendship, I have handled tragedies both without the true support of friends and community, and I have done it with them. And, yes, together is better.

Even the bad stuff is made better when we are in true community.

When my sister spent a summer fiercely battling septic shock, I went it alone. I did the bare minimum to alert people, but for the most part it was me, without community, in one of our family's scariest crises to date. This aloneness was entirely my own doing and ultimately the cause of my unraveling. As with welcoming the service of others in my life, I kept the walls high. The weight of that particular tragedy was heavy. My sister's healing is one of many miracles we have experienced, and she is alive and well today; however, my family and I came out of that period held together by a thread.

I have spent a lot of time reflecting on why that particular trial was hard for us to weather. We, as a family, have been through so many trials before and weathered them well. This one was different. I was working a lot, our marriage wasn't in a great place at the time, and those two things coupled with all my shame and fear of finding ourselves in yet another tragedy led me to isolation. That isolation proved to be the deciding factor in how I weathered the trial differently than before. Tragedy without community is heavy; the burdens are weightier when they fall on your shoulders alone.

At some point that summer, two friends got wind of how bad things were and called to tell me they were showing up in an hour with food for my family. They weren't asking if they could come by—they were coming. When they arrived, they stood in my kitchen and asked for every detail of how things were really going. They prayed over me and our family right then and there. And then one of them said, "I am worried about you. I have seen you walk through many hard things, and you have never looked like this." I was worn ragged. I was exhausted. I was not sleeping more than an hour or two each night. I had developed the need for an inhaler because I was having trouble breathing. No one knew until a few friends bravely came banging on my door.

By not welcoming others into my grief, I also created distance in those relationships. By protecting myself with isolation, I was actually isolating people who care about me—people who would have been there for me in deep community. Rather than binding us together, my tribulation created more distance. Have you ever heard that your close friend experienced something really hard after the fact? It stings. It is easy to feel hurt by that. It's as if you are not worthy of trust in that situation, or perhaps you weren't close enough to be let in. Within a Breaking Bread Community, we must make room for each other even in the hard places. This was a difficult lesson for me to learn.

Our family has faced new trials and tragedies since that time. Having learned my lesson, I no longer go it alone. I have included my friends wholly and without reservation. My community has been invited in every time. The burdens, even of Dad's sudden decline and passing, were far, far less than I could have ever imagined them to be. The only difference in how I handled these new tragedies is that I was surrounded by people who knew me and who stood alongside my family as we went through the valleys. Knowing we will be in positions of stress, facing trials and unexpected burdens, we need to be prepared to let our Breaking Bread Community in—not just because of the fellowship and the joy of serving and receiving service well, but because the weight of our grief is not meant for our shoulders alone.

As a friend within this type of deep community, the call is also on us to be willing to hold our friends' grief well. We are often "fixers" by nature. When friends are grieving, they don't need fixing at all. What is needed instead is a loving friend to stand in that space with them. To see them and acknowledge where they are. This may require us to reconsider our response to grieving friends. Coming alongside friends and standing in the gap with them is often all that is required in seasons of grief. The deep roots of friendship grab hold and offer stability when you do that for a friend.

Meeting people in their grief or trial often looks like listening, rather than problem solving, grieving with them rather than trying to eliminate the grief. This is hard! My friend Mary Ellen navigated this beautifully with me when I was in the midst of a medical emergency in our family. While I was busy updating everyone daily on the news, I was aware of all the people waiting on me to send them into action. Mary Ellen simply stood in the gap with me, expecting nothing of me. She put it on herself to check in with me and was so amazingly consistent with it.

I didn't realize how badly I needed that until it was given. After having learned of what was going on, her response was to check in and say to me, "You don't have to think about me at all. I will be here, and I will check in with you tomorrow at the same time to see how things are." She checked on me and made it known that she was there, steady and consistent. She put no responsibility on me, and it was such a relief to have someone who wasn't looking to me to equip them to help. During times of crisis, we all like to be busy as we struggle to control the uncontrollable. Mary Ellen's willingness to stay and let me know she was still in it without trying to fix anything was an incredible example. When our friend is heartbroken, then so are we. Our efforts to eradicate that grief are often misplaced and are actually a way for us to feel more comfortable. The beautiful truth, however, is that meeting a friend in sorrow and simply being with her can turn grief into joy for both of you.

How is that possible?

Grief is halved when it is shared. Imagine grief as a pile of bricks your friend is holding. If we start picking up the bricks and moving them or breaking them to bits, it isn't honoring the grief itself. Instead, if we have the ability to hold some of the bricks for our friend, the burden is lighter. That is the goal. A community based on love and abundance, humble service, and vulnerability, like a Breaking Bread Community, is made to handle grief.

MEET ME AT THE TABLE

John 16:33 reminds us that we are to expect sorrow, tribulation. We are to expect trials. We have already studied this verse within the context of the shame we may have for our imperfect, trial-filled lives. Now let's look closer at what else Jesus offers us in this verse.

> I have said these things to you, that in me you may have peace. In the world you will have tribulation. But take heart; I have overcome the world. (ESV)

Jesus promises us peace in him. When we are facing tribulation, peace can feel so far off, yet it is the thing we crave, isn't it? I have always found even the sound of the word *peace* to be so very peaceful. It sounds like an exhale for my stressed out, weary soul. Peace.

Peace is translated from the Greek word *eirēnē*. What is really interesting is the root word of *eirēnē* is *eiro*, which means "to join." Peace comes from joining. This is the peace Jesus offers us during tribulation. We are offered peace by joining with Jesus and seeking a relationship with him first and foremost. His peace is the primary gift for certain, but here is where things affect your job as a friend grieving or standing beside a grieving friend. One of the roles of our community, with our deepest friends, is to reflect Jesus. As we join together with our community for support, we get the peace amid tribulations that Christ promises us. The peace we seek is found in joining together. This is why isolation, while numbing, is not actually comforting. Isolation is literally the opposite of the peace we seek.

When our friends are hurting, we can be a vehicle of peace for them by simply joining in, standing in the gap with them. Standing in the gap with friends as they are grieving is important work. Be warned: we will likely get it wrong from time to time.

Meeting friends in their grief and trial will have us occasionally going too far and perhaps dropping the ball at other times. When you find yourself missing the mark, take heart, as you will be in the company of the disciples, and once again Jesus has a lesson for us the evening of the Last Supper.

> He took Peter, James and John along with him, and he began to be deeply distressed and troubled. "My soul is overwhelmed with sorrow to the point of death," he said to them. "Stay here and keep watch."
>
> Going a little farther, he fell to the ground and prayed that if possible the hour might pass from him. "*Abba*, Father," he said, "everything is possible for you. Take this cup from me. Yet not what I will, but what you will."
>
> Then he returned to his disciples and found them sleeping. "Simon," he said to Peter, "are you asleep? Couldn't you keep watch for one hour?" (Mark 14:33–37)

As we find ourselves in the Garden of Gethsemane on the night of the Last Supper, we see Jesus, distressed and full of sorrow. He asked his friends to keep watch, to stand in the gap. After praying by himself, he found his friends not keeping watch, but instead asleep. Talk about missing the mark! What Jesus had requested is something we all need when we are in distress, to know that our friends are with us, standing in the space of our distress and not wavering. And yet the disciples were simply not up to it. Two more times Jesus asked them to stay alert and pray for him, and two more times he found them sleeping (Mark 14:38–41).

Reflecting on the scene at Gethsemane, I am also reminded that while we call on our friends to stay alert, keep watch, stay vigilant in prayer, and stand in solidarity with us, none of this will bring us the comfort of time with the Father. Jesus knew this. He knew that it was good and right to ask his friends to be with him; he also knew they wouldn't get it right, and yet he sought their solidarity again. Ultimately, Christ knew where to go to receive the ultimate comfort. This is an important lesson for us as we realize that both grief and joy are always meant to be a part of our story.

> So also you have sorrow now, but I will see you again,
> and your hearts will rejoice, and no one will take your
> joy from you. (John 16:22 ESV)

The disciples, as a community, were about to experience a significant loss. By the end of this night, Jesus would be arrested, and by morning he would be sentenced to death on the cross. What was to follow was sorrow within their community in particular. Remember, we have the perspective of knowing the end of the story. We know that on the third day Jesus rose again. We already have the gift of perspective because we see the victory. The disciples did not have that viewpoint, and so Jesus was equipping his friends with a different perspective: there will be sorrow, but there will also be joy.

As Christ addressed his departure from the disciples, a loss that would be devastating to their community, he assured them that joy would be theirs when they reunited. Jesus affirmed both the importance of community and the everlasting joy found in Christ himself. When we are experiencing great sorrow within our community, we can look also for the joy. I have experienced a friend moving away that felt like a tremendous loss. There was a lot of grieving at that reality. And yet even within a cross-country move, there was a certainty that our friendship was not over. We would stay united and be reunited as often as we could with trips to her home, surprise visits, and our willingness to find new ways to connect over the many miles. And just as Jesus promised us, no one could take away the joy we had in friendship and community.

I cannot imagine how hard it must be to truly say goodbye to a dear friend who has passed. I have personally faced the loss of many loved ones but never the particular sorrow of losing a dear friend. My experiences with death have taught me that we truly can have the same perspective Jesus promises us. When we are united in Christ, there is a reunion coming that we can count on and look forward to. And oh! The joy that awaits.

The ability to hold both joy and sorrow simultaneously is a gift of community. We have room to be both grieving and hopeful, both sorrowful and full of joy. Two summers ago, the Birthday Club met for a special send-off celebration for one of our own. After months of praying and crying and celebrating and grieving and accepting and packing, it was time to send a dear friend across the country to where God had called her and her family. That night, sitting around the table, celebrating all that we had become as a group of women deeply committed to loving each other, it felt holy. We knew we had a few more days before the official goodbye, but this was our night, set aside to acknowledge the sorrow of the move and the complete joy it was to be together.

When I finally made it home late that night and crawled into my bed, drenched from a combination of torrential downpour and torrential tears shed, my husband asked me simply, "How did it go?" I found myself speechless. There was a pain in my gut so deep and a lump in my throat so big that I was silent for several minutes. When I was finally able to respond, I said, "It was beautiful. And then we cried. But we cried because it was beautiful."

Grief and joy.

BREAK BREAD TOGETHER

After studying God's Word, we will spend time reflecting, praying, and preparing to take action. Let's have our friendships transformed by our time in the Word!

1. Are there times you have isolated yourself during a trial or trying time?

2. What are ways you can more intentionally include your community in your grief?

3. Are you a fixer by nature? How can you walk with grieving friends without trying to fix things for them?

4. When faced with our own struggles or seasons of grief, how can we also remember that joy is promised to us?

Father,

We know that we are promised tribulations in this world. When we are facing them, would you point us to your perspective? Help us to remember that you have already claimed the victory, Lord, and that in relationship with you we can experience grief that turns to joy. When our friends are hurting, Lord, use us as a means to reflect your joy back to them. Help us to sit together in the trials, holding each other's grief and halving the weight of the burden. May we remember that grief is not ours to bear alone. You have designed us for community, and our communities are made to point us to you and to offer us joy. We are so thankful. Amen, indeed.

CHAPTER FIFTEEN

COMMUNITY OF LOVE

I love my friends. I love them so deeply and truly that sometimes it takes my breath away. It is a totally different love than I feel for my family. A love that I didn't really believe existed. There is a solidarity and companionship found in my community that feels simply too good to be true. And yet, it is. It is a community of love.

I never thought I wanted friendships like this. My family—my husband and my kids—are the most important people in the world to me. I could not understand how someone could be a great mom and wife and also have friends that she loved as much as I love my friends. It felt selfish to me. But the type of community and friendships we have been studying, the example so clearly laid out for us at the Last Supper, is a different kind of friendship. There is nothing selfish about making room in your life for this kind of friendship. As we have really looked at how friendships like this play out, it has become evident that this is not your average friendship.

When you have the honor of living in a Breaking Bread Community, you too will feel it. There is immeasurable trust and comfort. You are truly known and seen and loved for exactly who you are. There is freedom in friendship like that, just as there is freedom within Christ himself who knows you and sees you and loves you for who you are. The freedom is breathtaking. It allows you to open yourself up and sacrifice yourself. It allows you to forgive and repent. It allows you to break bread together, with grace and love and mercy, understanding and compassion.

When you have the honor of simply witnessing a Breaking Bread Community, you will feel it as well. Even from the outside, you can tell there is something different. A special type of bond appears when friendship is based on this type of love. These communities filled with prayed-for friends who are vulnerable with each other, who serve each other, who speak life into and over each other, who sit with each other through grief and joy, who are steadfast and true, even when hurt—they are different! Here is what you need to be prepared for: other people will notice your friendship.

When women are truly supporting and loving on each other, when they show up for each other in this way, people take notice. And when they want to know what is different about your friendship, you will be able to point them to the difference: friendship based on Jesus's example. The encouragement, trust, and intimacy that is apparent in Breaking Bread Communities is so compelling to the broken world. The freedom in being truly known and loved shines through the way friends like this interact. Love pours out of us and into each other with total abundance.

People in my life have met Jesus when they began to notice the beauty and depth of love in my friendships. They recognized that something was different. The difference is that we truly love each other as Christ loves. There is no better testimony than that. Just as when we spend time with Jesus in community with him, our love for one another will spill out and bless those around us when we spend time together in a Breaking Bread Community. As I mentioned way back in the beginning of this book, our other relationships will thrive. Even more than that, we will experience a missional outpouring that comes from our having intercepted with Christ and this Christlike community.

MEET ME AT THE TABLE

The love we are being called to is no small thing. At its heart a Breaking Bread Community, a community of love is the highest calling. As Christ himself says, "Greater love has no one than this."

> My command is this: Love each other as I have loved you. Greater love has no one than this: to lay down one's life for one's friends. . . .
>   You did not choose me, but I chose you and appointed you so that you might go and bear fruit— fruit that will last—and so that whatever you ask in my name the Father will give you. This is my command: Love each other. (John 15:12–13, 16–17)

As someone who can be seen as cold or standoffish, I want to acknowledge that this level of love can be intimidating. I was never a big hugger. I did not easily share my emotions with others. And somehow that became my identity. Another wall-building technique. Well, somewhere along the way, I realized that all these people in my life needed to know how much I valued them. Likely this came from one too many trials facing death of a loved one.

As I began to intentionally build my Breaking Bread Community, going deep with the ones I prayed for and God chose, I decided to just get over myself. "I love you" became an easy thing to say. Hugs, warm and welcome, blessedly became more and more a part of how I connected with my friends. I decided to love big and let it be known.

This is the kind of love Jesus himself demonstrated and then called us to as well. And, friends, it is just so much better this way. What did I have to gain by holding back with these people? Absolutely nothing. My love for these people is so vast, and I believe it is because it is modeled after the vastness of the love that Jesus has for me and for you. Therefore, if I were to hold back on expressing the fullness of the love I have for these special friendships, I would be minimizing the love of Jesus himself.

As we sat at our Birthday Club, we were reflecting on the first full year of celebrations and community in this intentional way. There was a shift occurring. It was tangible. We were being equipped. This was November of 2017, and I looked around the table of my beloved friends and proclaimed, "God is going to do something. I feel it. There is a reason he brought us together, and I think a year from now, we will be able to see it." Of all my friends, I am the least prophetic; however, that sense was dead-on.

Within two months, we had created a new ministry whose sole purpose is to gather women of the northeast together, to encourage them and to send them back to their homes on fire for the Lord. Come on. Seasons Northeast wasn't even a thought in November, and by the end of January it had a name, a mission, and a trajectory that could only come from God himself. Seasons has gone on to host four events a year with women from more than seventy-five churches in one of the top five most unchurched areas of the country. God is good. This is a perfect example of fruit that will last. Breaking Bread Communities, when walking out the full example of Christ and the disciples, can't help but produce good fruit. But it is the *fully* walking out that will bring the abundance and therefore the fruit. When we as a community fully exemplify Christ and his love, we get to participate in community as afforded by Christ.

As we begin to understand the impact of these friendships and communities as they interact with the world, I want to take us away from the Last Supper to a passage in the letter of Hebrews to reflect on the impact of our communities and what happens when we gather.

> But you have come to Mount Zion and to the city of the living God, the heavenly Jerusalem, and to innumerable angels in festal gathering, and to the assembly of the firstborn who are enrolled in heaven, and to God, the judge of all, and to the spirits of the righteous made perfect, and to Jesus, the mediator of a new covenant, and to the sprinkled blood that speaks a better word than the blood of Abel. (Heb. 12:22–24 ESV)

This section of Hebrews serves as a reminder to the believers that we, as a community, participate in the new thing Jesus accomplished. The good news is that when we come together in community, we gather not just with each other but also with multitudes of angels, the heirs of the kingdom (the firstborns), spirits of those made perfect, and even Jesus himself. How amazing! This is why Breaking Bread Communities have such power!

Fully stepping into this kind of community allows us to partake in the heavenly community, today. Not only that, but what we do with our community here reflects heaven for others to see. As we take part in an everlasting community, we have an everlasting impact.

This passage also offers great encouragement to us as we are reminded that the type of friendships we are building are eternal! As heirs of the kingdom, we are the firstborn and therefore in everlasting community with each other and in eternal fellowship with God. The joy of community is that we don't have to wait until heaven to participate in the new work of Jesus. Our friendships fully allow us to experience this type of community, here and now.

Our world needs this kind of friendship on display as an example of how very much we are all loved by the Savior of the World. Imagine a world where others see our friendships and the love that pours out of them as a tangible reminder of the love of Jesus. We would have a friendship revival on our hands. It's possible! Join us. Come, let's break bread together.

BREAK BREAD TOGETHER

After studying God's Word, we will spend time reflecting, praying, and preparing to take action. Let's have our lives transformed by our time in the Word!

1. What differences can you see in the community we have explored and the ones prevalent in our culture today?

2. How can you consistently demonstrate your love for your friends?

3. How can you demonstrate Jesus's love for the world through your friendships?

4. Can you imagine how living out this type of community can bring others to know Jesus?

Father,

You are a God of love. When we look at these friendships we are building, help us to fully see your love in us and pouring out of us. We want our friendships to look different, Lord. We want our friendships and communities to be marked by you and your love. If we are known for nothing else, let us, as a community, be known for how we love each other, the world around us, and you. Amen, indeed.

RESOURCES

Beyond the information and questions throughout this book, I have created even more resources for going deeper in your study and for sharing *Break Bread Together* with your communities. To download the bonus resources listed below, visit www.BreakBreadTogetherBook.com.

May you find true friendship and deep community with those around you and with Christ himself.

PERSONAL STUDY GUIDE

Dig deeper into *Break Bread Together* with this guide that includes word studies, additional Scripture, journaling prompts, and more. If you enjoyed the references to Greek and Hebrew or found yourself wanting more time and space to process each chapter, this study guide is for you!

LEADER'S GUIDE

Lead a discussion group or book club! This leader's guide walks you through eight sessions of group discussion questions, background and cultural history to round out your discussion, and tangible ways to implement the principles of *Break Bread Together* within the group as well as tips on what to anticipate within a group study.

LAST SUPPER CELEBRATE AND REMEMBER GUIDE

Walk your friends and family through a Passover celebration that points to Jesus. This comprehensive guide includes narration, Scripture, celebration setup, and even a grocery list and recipes!

ACKNOWLEDGMENTS

I have been blessed by many friendships throughout my life. I am so thankful for how they shaped me and how they pointed me back to a God who cares for me. The names in this book are real people who have had tremendous influence on me, and for each one I am so thankful.

BDC: Amy—for dreaming big with me every morning and running on mission with me like only God could have us do; Heather—for encouraging me to make the hard choices and having met me in some of my darkest moments with love and grace; Jen—for inspiring me and offering your friendship as one of the sweetest gifts I have ever received; Kathy—for your adventurous spirit and lighthearted way of making heavy burdens feel so much lighter; Kristen—for equipping me to pursue Jesus deeper and for seeing God's beauty in all. There is no book without all of you, but even more I am different for your having loved me so well.

Allie: My truest friend. You are steadfast and kind beyond measure. My life is better for having you in it and for having you here for so very long.

MEMcQ: For being my first editor and the very best steward of the hope of this book in the very beginning. You love us all so well.

Seasons BoD: To see what God is doing through our community is an absolute joy! As Reneé said, and I always quote, "I can't believe we get to do this!"

BBT prayer team: You have held me and this book baby up in prayer for two years. So very thankful for your hearts, your petitions, and your friendship.

SHS girls: I never thought our friendships after high school would be bound by so much loss and grief and trial. No one else knows the specific burdens like you do. What a club to be in, but I'm so thankful I have you.

Loudonville Community Church, our home for the last dozen years: I am so thankful for the community we found there. Pastor Paul, thank you for being such an amazing teacher and student of the Word, and thank you for your generous sharing of wisdom throughout the writing process.

The hope*writers community: Joining h*w was the start of my journey as a writer. The resources and education I found there changed my trajectory, and I am forever thankful. Your willingness to pour into writers has made such a difference in my life. I was equipped because of you. To my h*w author group, thank you for the safe space to work our way through publishing together with openness and community.

My agent, Blythe Daniel: I am indebted. Our first meeting was a dream come true. Your support and expertise push me to do better. Thank you for believing in me first!

The Leafwood Publishers team: We prayed for the right publisher to find this book, and I am so thankful for this partnership. You have given freedom and guidance to make this message what it is: a bold declaration of the goodness of kingdom living on earth and in heaven. Thank you.

My family: I love you. We have been through so much, and I am so proud of us! To my kiddos, who have watched Mom stay up late, wake up early, squeeze in moments of work where I can, thank you for your patience and for being my biggest cheerleaders.

Josh: Nothing happens without you. For saying yes a million times, for being the one who keeps me on track, for being the one who sees missional opportunities when I am weighed down with the work, for loving me so well through all.

s.d.g.